# LOVE-POWERED PARENTING

**Other Resources by Tom Holladay**

*Foundations* (coauthored with Kay Warren)

*The Relationship Principles of Jesus*

# LOVE-POWERED PARENTING

## LOVING YOUR KIDS THE WAY JESUS LOVES YOU

## TOM & CHAUNDEL HOLLADAY

### FOREWORD BY RICK & KAY WARREN

ZONDERVAN®

ZONDERVAN.com/
AUTHORTRACKER
*follow your favorite authors*

ZONDERVAN

*Love-Powered Parenting*
Copyright © 2011 by Tom Holladay

This title is also available as a Zondervan ebook.
Visit www.zondervan.com/ebooks.

This title is also available in a Zondervan audio edition.
Visit www.zondervan.fm.

Requests for information should be addressed to:

Zondervan, *Grand Rapids, Michigan 49530*

ISBN 978-0-310-33505-4

International Trade Paper Edition

*Cover illustration: iStockphoto®*
*Interior illustration: iStockphoto®*
*Interior design: Beth Shagene*

*Printed in the United States of America*

11 12 13 14 15 16 17 /DCI/ 22 21 20 19 18 17 16 15 14 13 12 11 10 9 8 7 6 5 4 3 2 1

*To Ryan, Alyssa, and Luke*
*with grateful hearts for the joy of being your parents*

# Contents

PARENTING PRINCIPLE #6

# Live the Golden Rule
## The Power of Your Unselfishness

# Foreword
# by Rick and Kay Warren

There is no more important responsibility in life than that of being a parent.

Our communities, our churches, and our cultures are always only one generation away from destruction. If parents do not pass on the wisdom and character lessons of previous generations, we fail to leave the legacy God repeatedly commands us to leave with our children.

In Deuteronomy 6:5–7, God commands:

> "Love the LORD your God with all your heart and with all your soul and with all your strength. These commandments that I give you today are to be upon your hearts. Impress them on your children. Talk about them when you sit at home and when you walk along the road, when you lie down and when you get up."

This passage clearly teaches that parenting is a full-time job, regardless of your career. You may take time off from your job, but you are never "off the clock" when it comes to parenting. This passage also explains that the first and primary task of parenting is to teach our children to love God supremely.

It is not enough to raise your kids in church; you must raise them in Christ!

Fortunately, what you hold in your hand is a field manual for the task. Tom and Chaundel Holladay have given us a book filled with insights on the critical task of parenting that are biblically based, practically useful, and time-tested. Since Tom is the senior teaching pastor at Saddleback Church, and since Chaundel grew up in a pastor's family, this book has special relevance to parents involved in church ministry. They understand the special needs and pressures of raising children in a fishbowl.

This is no ivory tower theory of parenting. The advice comes from a lifetime of raising kids and helping thousands of others do the same. Read it, underline it, discuss it, apply it, and let it strengthen your family as you grow in the grace of the Lord!

RICK AND KAY WARREN,
Lake Forest, California

# Introduction

I love being a dad. The two most difficult times of spiritual discouragement in my life have been when we were told we may not be able to have children (God had different plans) and when we saw our first child leave home for college. Maybe it's that I wanted to improve on a less-than-perfect relationship with my dad; maybe it's an appreciation for God's miracle of creation; or maybe it's the deep sense of fulfillment that comes when things go right—I love being a dad.

*I love being a mom. Long before Tom and I were engaged, while still in college, I thought through the whole issue of whether I should even have children or not. It was in the day of much discussion about the population explosion, and many people were questioning whether it was right to bring a child into our mixed-up, overcrowded world. There were many children around the world (as there are now) needing adoption. I had an innate desire to get married and raise a family, but I intentionally took a step back and questioned the true purpose and reason behind my desire. At least for a moment, I was willing to consider sacrificing my plans and my desire (which I believed were God-given) unless there was a significant purpose or outcome of having my own children.*

*Tom and I were taking a class in discipleship at college. As I thought and prayed through this issue, I realized that having children was the ultimate discipleship experience. To take a human being "from scratch" and seek to love, nurture, mold, and change them, cooperating with God to guide them to become conformed to Christ's image, was the perfect opportunity for intense discipleship training. The fact that God could use me, imperfect as I was and knowing I would be an imperfect parent, to contribute toward populating his world with true disciples was a thrilling opportunity.*

*Great risks were involved in this ultimate discipleship project, as is true in any discipleship relationship. There was the possibility I would invest my life for years, only to have my child choose not to follow God. It was a risk I was willing to take.*

We love being parents! This encouragement resource for parents is written out of that love. Yes, there are experiences in parenting that can cause deep hurt. Yes, there are realities in parenting that certainly will cause a person to feel inept. Yet at the core of it all, there is deep gratefulness for the gift God gives in the opportunity to love a child, as well as great appreciation for the grace God gives to grow in our parenting.

We say with great apprehension that this book is intended to be a biblical guide to parenting. The apprehension comes not from the truth of the Bible but from the heavy-handed or trite way we sometimes express this truth. When it comes to difficult issues like parenting, we know we don't have all the answers and can hope that if we shout Bible verses loud enough, it will seem like we do!

By "biblical guide," we mean these pages are intended to take all of us on a journey through what God's Word has to say about parenting. Our main goal will not be to uncover psychological truths about our children at their particular age and stage. Don't mistake our meaning. We firmly believe that psychology and educational theory have much to teach us about parenting. Yet it is the simple and profound principles of God's Word that help us distinguish psychological truth from error, educational reality from untested theory.

Neither will our goal be centered only on practical tips for every circumstance. There are already many good resources on such things as how to get kids to eat their green beans without sticking them up their noses and how to get your children through a cross-state car ride to Grandma's without destroying your sanity. While we cannot write about parenting without grasping this bull by the horn (or green bean by the end), we'll be looking at these tips within the broader context of God's principles for parenting.

On a personal note, if we are ever going to write a book about parenting, now is the time. Luke, our third of three children, is leaving home for college in the year we are writing this, and our first grandchild will be born by the time it is completed. So, while we still face the daily realities of parenting and before we move completely into the blissfully and intentionally less complicated world of grandparenting, our love for children and for parents and families makes this writing a true calling for us.

Every line in this book is essentially written by both of us because of our influence on each other over the years of parenting. However, for simplicity's sake, Tom's voice will lead us through the main portions of each chapter, and Chaundel's voice will close each chapter with a brief response. So if you want the greatest wisdom, just read the responses at the end! (Tom wrote that last sentence.)

You'll notice that the book is written as a thirty-day journey. We tend to learn more by reading thirty short segments over thirty days than by sitting down to absorb something in just one or two readings. Besides, as a parent you only have time for a short daily reading! We encourage you to read one chapter a day over thirty days; reading these chapters together as parents would be even better. If you're a single parent, find a friend who will read along with you and meet for coffee or at the park once a week to talk about what God is saying to you.

• • •

The principles in this book are based on the six principles of love modeled in the life of Jesus—principles I explored in my book *The Relationship Principles of Jesus*. In reading through the Gospels again and again with a mind toward what Jesus did and said about relationships, these principles were clear.

## RELATIONSHIP PRINCIPLE #1: Place the Highest Value on Relationships

"The most important command is this: 'Listen, people of Israel! The Lord our God is the only Lord. Love the Lord your God with all your heart, all your soul, all your mind, and all your strength.' The second command is this: 'Love your neighbor as you love yourself.' There are no commands more important than these."

MARK 12:29–31 NCV

RELATIONSHIP PRINCIPLE #2: **Love as Jesus Loves You**

> "A new command I give you: Love one another. As I have loved you, so you must love one another."
>
> JOHN 13:34

RELATIONSHIP PRINCIPLE #3: **Communicate from the Heart**

> "For out of the overflow of the heart the mouth speaks."
>
> MATTHEW 12:34

RELATIONSHIP PRINCIPLE #4: **As You Judge, You Will Be Judged**

> "Do not judge, or you too will be judged. For in the same way you judge others, you will be judged, and with the measure you use, it will be measured to you."
>
> MATTHEW 7:1–2

RELATIONSHIP PRINCIPLE #5: **The Greatest Are the Servants**

> "The greatest among you will be your servant. For whoever exalts himself will be humbled, and whoever humbles himself will be exalted. "
>
> MATTHEW 23:11–12

RELATIONSHIP PRINCIPLE #6: **Treat Others as You Want Them to Treat You**

> "Do to others as you would have them do to you."
>
> LUKE 6:31

Even a quick glance at these principles shows how powerfully and specifically they apply to parenting. In this book we will explore how these principles fit into our lives as parents. Our prayer is that the teaching and example of Jesus will become clear and relevant to you as we explore these six principles we can apply as parents.

PARENTING PRINCIPLE #1
## Believe Nothing Is More Important
The Power of Your Priorities

PARENTING PRINCIPLE #2
## Love with New Power
The Power of Your Love

PARENTING PRINCIPLE #3
## Communicate from the Heart
The Power of Your Words

PARENTING PRINCIPLE #4
## Show and Teach Mercy
The Power of Your Discipline and Compassion

PARENTING PRINCIPLE #5
## Serve Your Children Well
The Power of Your Serving

PARENTING PRINCIPLE #6
## Live the Golden Rule
The Power of Your Unselfishness

If your family is just beginning, have faith! God is about to do something wonderful in and through your lives as you set out on the faith adventure of parenting.

If your family is struggling, have hope! There is no such thing as a perfect family, and nothing on this side of heaven is without problems. Yet God is in the business of change.

A lot of families are like antique furniture. The beauty is still there, hidden underneath the dust of silence and the cobwebs of past hurts. Every family needs restoration from time to time. Someone needs to strip off the old, cracked finish to reveal the natural beauty underneath; a few squirts of oil are needed for rusty hinges on doors that have remained closed for too long. Hope gives us the power to look to God for restoration.

Whatever your family is like, have love! The power of God's love, even in those times when you can't seem to sense it, is more real than anything else in your life. God is willing to give you that power to love in any and every circumstance your family faces. Our prayer is that you will experience his love in amazing ways during these next thirty days.

TOM AND CHAUNDEL HOLLADAY

# Believe Nothing Is More Important

## The Power of Your Priorities

Then little children were brought to Jesus for him to place his hands on them and pray for them. But the disciples rebuked those who brought them.

Jesus said, "Let the little children come to me, and do not hinder them, for the kingdom of heaven belongs to such as these."

Matthew 19:13–14

# The Priority of Love

Parenting is a relationship. Anyone who has been a parent for more than a day knows how easily we can turn this relationship of parenting into merely a task. Bottle dispensed, diaper changed, asleep in crib — my parenting tasks are done for the day. Eighteen years later, it's schoolwork finished, dinner fed, in by curfew — the day's parenting tasks are over. Parenting is filled with tasks, but the task is never the most important part of parenting. Parenting is a relationship.

Jesus taught us that when we look at the whole of life, nothing is more important than relationships. So it clearly follows that when we look at parenting, nothing is more important than the relationships — my relationship with God and my relationship with my children.

Coming to realize that it is not the skill or task of parenting that is most important but rather the relationship is extremely encouraging in light of one of the realities we all face: we're often not very good at parenting! A number of years ago, when our three children were from early preschool to early grade school age, I decided to take them all shopping together for Mother's Day—to an antique store. I thought, "This will be no problem." What was I thinking! The expensive vases and china teacups and fragile wood furniture cowered in their places just seeing us enter the store—and every shopping mother and grandmother looked at me with terror in their eyes. I believe we made it out without any major damage to the antiques, but the strain of the experience exhausted us for days. There is something about actual parenting that humbles you. This is why Charlie Shedd's famous story on the challenges of parenting resonates with us. Before he had children, he boldly preached on "How to Raise Your Children." After he became a parent, the message became "Some Suggestions to Parents"—and with two more children, it changed to "Feeble Hints to Fellow Strugglers."*

Successfully navigating the difficult waters of parenting starts with a clear priority: *nothing is more important than love*. That's the truth to remember anytime you wonder whether what you are doing as a parent is important. In a world that too often values tasks over relationships, the truth Jesus taught tells us it is the relationships that are most important. When Jesus was asked by a teacher of the law to name the most important commandment, he immediately replied, "'Love the Lord your God with all your heart and with all your soul and with all your mind and with all your strength.' The second is this: 'Love your neighbor as yourself.' There is no commandment greater than these" (Mark 12:30–31). Love God and love people; there is nothing you do that is more important.

What does this mean for us as parents? It means par-

---

*Charlie Shedd, *Promises to Peter* (Waco, Tex.: Word, 1970), 7.

enting is a priority! And it means love is a priority in our parenting.

You can see the priority of parenting in the way Jesus treated children. Remember the day a group of mothers took their children to see Jesus? Imagine the energy and excitement in this crowd—moms and kids gathering more mothers with their children as they walked down the street toward a single purpose: "We're going to see Jesus!" Think of how it must have felt as the mothers shared with their children the anticipation of meeting this man they had heard so much about. "Jesus is a man who cares about people like us. They say he does miracles and heals people. He teaches in ways even children can understand. Many even say Jesus is the Promised One of God we have been waiting for. We're going to see Jesus for you, little one. I want Jesus to pray for you. I want this man of God to bless you."

They finally catch a glimpse of Jesus in the square far down the narrow street. The mothers walk a little faster, and the children's chatter grows more excited. They're getting close enough for Jesus to hear them now. The mothers begin to cry out his name; they gather their children into their arms to prepare to present them to Jesus.

Just a few feet away from Jesus now—and suddenly the disciples of Jesus stand in their way. "Stop!" they say. "Jesus doesn't have time for the children. You'll have to take them away." The mothers stand stunned, not knowing what to do. Then they turn to walk away. "I'm sorry, sweetheart. We won't be able to see Jesus today." Tears of disappointment begin to fall from the children's eyes; cries of "Why can't we, Mommy?" escape from their lips. At this very moment of letdown, they hear a rich, gentle, powerful voice speaking. "Do not prevent the little children from coming to me." Turning back, they are greeted by the welcoming smile and open arms of Jesus. (From Matthew 19:13–15.)

• • •

Like these busy disciples, many people in our busy world act as if what you are doing is unimportant. But Jesus' actions affirm the priority of your parenting. There are three specific choices you can make to encourage a growing sense of the priority of what you do as a mom or dad: accept parenting as a calling, prepare your life for parenting, and value your role as a parent.

First, you remind yourself that parenting is more than a set of tasks; it is a life calling. How do you know if you're called to be a parent? If you have a child, you are called!

You may say, "I didn't plan this—at least not this many kids or not in this timing." If you have children, clearly you have been called by God, your children's creator, to be a parent. Whatever the circumstances of your child's birth, the miracle of their birth is all the evidence you need that you have been called by God. There is an awesome power in recognizing that you are called—the power to live up to the priorities God has now placed in your life. Paul wrote, "I ... beg you to lead a life worthy of your calling, for you have been called by God" (Ephesians 4:1 NLT). You "lead a life worthy" of being a parent, not in order to get called, but because you know you *are* called.

Second, the priority of parenting is encouraged as you prepare to be the best parent you can be. We invest in preparation, training, and tools for any other career; it should be even more so with this most important of careers. You are shaping the next generation. Solomon writes, "Children are a gift from the LORD; they are a reward from him" (Psalm 127:3 NLT). They are a gift and a reward that require our time and energy. The time you spend reading a book or gaining wisdom from other parents will have a multiplied impact in your children's lives. Some of us learn best by reading, others by listening. However you best learn, it is important to learn from others. "People learn from one another, just as iron sharpens iron" (Proverbs 27:17 TEV). Get in a support group of parents; maybe even talk to grandparents. If you're reading this book, it shows you are motivated to prepare.

Let me share with you the two best words of advice about preparing to be a parent I've heard over the years. First, prepare for the good times, not just the tough times. Make no mistake, when you take the time to prepare a fun family vacation or to prepare to celebrate a milestone in your child's life, you are doing some of the best parenting you will ever do. Second, become comfortable with the fact that even the best-prepared parents are often unprepared. How could we be prepared for some of the things our kids throw at us? We never could have imagined they would decide to climb that, or jump from there, or think up that plan. Your preparation for parenting cannot prevent the chaos, but it can give you a measure of peace and even wisdom in the midst of the storm. Great parenting is not about building a perfectly ordered world; it is about knowing how to get your kids into the cellar when the tornado hits.

There is a third way to encourage your heart in the priority of parenting: remember the value of what you are doing. "So, my dear brothers and sisters, be strong and steady, always enthusiastic about the Lord's work, for you know that nothing you do for the Lord is ever useless" (1 Corinthians 15:58 NLT). Every work you do for God is of great value, and parenting is certainly God's work! Never forget the almost incalculable value of what you do. A world that measures value in tasks completed and money earned too often forgets the *real* bottom line is that people will last and things will not.

Linda Weber writes about a woman named Donna, who happened to be seated next to the CEO at her husband's company dinner. He asked her, "What do you do?" After learning she was a career mom of three preschoolers, the CEO turned away and spent the evening talking to the person on the other side of him. Linda's opinion: "Donna should have told Mr. Big she was director of health, education, and welfare. She should have said she was secretary of the treasury and the head of public affairs. She should have told him she was chairman of the house rules committee. She should have responded, 'I'm responsible to teach my kids everything from how to chew food to how to drive a car. What do *you* do all day?'"*

What happens when you hear these three encouragements from God to accept your calling, prepare your life, and value your role as a parent? You don't automatically get perfect kids or even become a perfect parent. But you do get a sense of the love of God that you need as a thread of hope on your toughest days, as a burst of strength on your most exhausting days, and as a higher purpose on even your best days.

---

*Linda Weber, *Mom, You're Incredible!* (Nashville: Broadman, 1999), 21–22.

### Response from the Heart of a Mom

*As a stay-at-home mom, I've had to continually remind myself of the value of my "career" choice. In doing ministry or running a home-based business, it is easier to see the immediate value of what I'm doing, but parenting is what God has called me to. It helps me to remember that it is a calling—an extremely valuable calling.*

WEEK 1, DAY 1: **The Priority of Love**

- **Verse to remember:** "I ... beg you to lead a life worthy of your calling, for you have been called by God" (Ephesians 4:1 NLT).

- **Action to take:** Accept God's encouragement of the value of your parenting.

- **Tomorrow:** Priorities begin with my choice.

# Priorities Begin with My Choice

I was talking with Chaundel recently about a commitment she had made a number of years ago concerning our youngest child, Luke. In her words, "After we dropped off our daughter, Alyssa, for college and came home, I felt sorry for Luke that he was now facing five years with just his parents. There was a part of me that was ready to move on with life, and it was a real temptation to act like we were done with parenting. Because Luke didn't demand a lot of attention for himself, I realized it would be easy to coast. I decided instead to be intentional in investing time and thought in parenting him rather than depending on him to get by on what we had already taught him. That decision to invest instead of coast was a decision that resulted in a great deal of unexpected joy in the building of our relationship."

As we look at the priority of love this week, we will focus these next three days on the three essentials that create a priority: your choice, your goals, and your time. Priorities begin with your choice, are expressed in your goals, and are accomplished in your time. We begin today with the truth that *priorities start with a choice*.

Relationships don't slide into a position of higher priority; we have to *make* them a priority. Money can slip into a place of greater importance in your life; success can, and even hobbies can—but not relationships. Relationships must be chosen as a priority, and then re-chosen and re-chosen and re-chosen. Because we tend to take each other for granted or to avoid the hard work of relationships, what was most important can easily become less important and sometimes even slip to unimportant. The priority of relationships must be a daily choice.

We all want to make this daily choice as parents— certainly this is true for anyone who has picked up this book. So what gets in the way? What keeps us from actually making a priority of something we *want* to be a priority? We've talked to too many parents who look back with regret on the time they didn't spend with their kids to think this couldn't happen to us.

I see three major obstacles that can get in the way of our making relationships a priority: decisions, distractions, and drift.

First, our own decisions can get in the way. Our relationship with our kids stops being a priority when we decide to make other things the priority. Perhaps it is a job or a hobby or some entertainment or even a ministry. Of course parents have to spend time at work, so please, no guilt trips here about the reality of balancing busy schedules. I'm talking about going on a business trip for days without connecting with or even thinking about your family. You are then deciding that something else is a higher priority. Sometimes we tell ourselves we're doing this "just for a time" or "just until things settle down." Have you discovered yet that the right time for relationships never comes and that things never settle down?

God leaves absolutely no doubt as to his opinion of the value and importance of parenting. If you ever come across someone who acts as if what you are doing for your family has little importance, point them to 1 Timothy 5:8: "If anyone does not provide for his relatives, and especially for his immediate family, he has denied the faith and is worse than an unbeliever." In fact, God says clearly that family is an even greater priority than church ministry. Consider these words about a group of widows who were spending their time serving God in the church: "These should learn first of all to put their religion into practice by caring for their own family and so repaying their parents and grandparents, for this is pleasing to God" (1 Timothy 5:4). Focus on these phrases: "these should learn first of all ... by caring for their own family." *First* is a priority word! God is telling us we may not hide from the priority of parenting, even in as important an activity as ministry in the church.

I will never forget hearing Billy Graham being interviewed by David Frost years ago. Frost asked the evangelist, who had seen so many God-honoring successes in his ministry, if his time away had shortchanged his family, and Billy Graham's humble answer was, "It did. I don't think any of my children would say that. But I feel it. I feel the emptiness of not being as much of a confidant that I would like to be to my children."* At age ninety, when asked in an interview for *Christianity Today* if he had any regrets, Graham said, "I regret that I didn't spend more time with my

---

*David Frost, *Billy Graham: Personal Thoughts of a Public Man* (Colorado Springs: Victor, 1997), 147.

family; I'm sure Ruth and the children paid a heavy price for all the times I was absent."*

We have to be careful, of course, not to make the opposite mistake and hide from ministry to others inside the comfortable cocoon of our family. *First* means something else must come second, which is to take care of the needs of hurting people. Don't use hurting people as an excuse for not taking care of your family, and don't use your family as an excuse for not caring for hurting people. These twin priorities of family first and then others are vital to achieving balance in a family. I've seen many families miss out by emphasizing just one of these two priorities. Some spend all of their time on family, only to realize that when the kids get older, they become self-centered because the only model they've seen is that they are the center of the universe. Others react against this to the extent that the needs of their family come ninth or tenth on the to-do list for the day, and therefore rarely if ever get attention. It's not a matter of serving my family or serving the world; it comes down to maintaining a crucial balance of both!

To make relationships a priority, we have to realize that our own decisions can get in the way when we let lesser things take the place of love in our lives. We also must be alert to two even more common and certainly more insidious enemies of the priority of parenting: distractions and drift. Distractions happen in the moment, and drift happens over time. These seemingly insignificant things can steal from us that which is most important. I am amazed at how hard I have to fight the distractions of little things like a fly on the wall or a thought in my head in order to

---

*Tim Funk, "Q&A: Billy Graham at 90," *Christianity Today*: www.christianity today.com/ct/2008/novemberweb-only/145-52.0.html.

stay relationally connected to those around me. It's shocking how far apart we can drift without really seeing it. I would love to begin a long discussion of theology here, but suffice it to say that because we live in a fallen world, the daily distractions and the natural drift of life tend to push us away from the priorities of love for God and others.

One of the most powerful ways to resist distractions and drift is to decide to *parent intentionally* instead of reactively. Reactive parenting is swerving to miss the rocks in the road; intentional parenting is planning to take a different route because you know that stretch of road is dangerous. Intentionality means such things as

- having a bedtime routine that includes snuggling, reading, and praying;
- making it a practice to stop and talk whenever you get good news from your child;
- asking specific questions about their day when you first see your child in the afternoon or evening;
- making it a habit to get them involved with you in projects around your home; and
- planning your evenings of entertainment together.

At its core, intentionality means *you make the relationship the priority*. Chaundel and I were recently doing something with one of our children, and we had gotten a late start to our destination and ran into heavy traffic on the way. I had an appointment looming, and I could feel the anxiety and rush beginning to swallow up our time together. After stressing about this for a few minutes, I grabbed my phone, made a call, and moved the appointment—and we ended up having a great time together. I'd like to say this is something

I do every time I get that pressured feeling, but I'd be lying. But when I do, or when I commit to another time for us to get together if the appointment can't be moved, I'm intentionally making the relationship the priority.

It can be an encouragement to avoid confusing intentionality with personality. Some of us are more spontaneous; others are better at keeping to the plan. Intentionality can happen in either case—both in the moment by determining in advance what you will do when the opportunities arise and in the schedule by writing down your plans in advance.

My problem with intentionality is that you have to be so intentional about it! The secret to being intentional over the long haul is in the principle we're learning from Jesus this week: *Nothing is more important than love.* Instead of beginning with a desire to better schedule your time with your children or to be more intentional in your parenting, begin with the decision to make love the priority. It may sound like a very small difference, but you will be amazed at the new strength and energy you'll find as a parent when you make the priority of love your daily beginning point.

### Response from the Heart of a Mom

*It has always been a lot of work for me to parent intentionally rather than reactively. The old saying "The squeaky wheel gets the grease" is true for me—and usually the loudest squeak wasn't coming from my children. Sometimes it was my list of tasks to be done; other times it was the call from a woman in crisis while I was making dinner or helping with homework. I have found too often that the important parts of parenting never seemed urgent. I love it when I have taken the time to plan ahead and write down in my weekly schedule specific times for getting together with each of our children. The results are phenomenal. Preventative maintenance is a lot more fun and less costly too.*

WEEK 1, DAY 2: **Priorities Begin with My Choice**

- **Verse to remember:** "These should learn first of all to put their religion into practice by caring for their own family and so repaying their parents and grandparents, for this is pleasing to God" (1 Timothy 5:4).

- **Action to take:** Look or plan for one way you can parent intentionally today.

- **Tomorrow:** Priorities are expressed in my goals.

# Priorities Are Expressed in My Goals

One of the keys to living out the priority of love in your parenting is settling in your own mind what you are aiming for as a parent. Some parents aim too high, determining that if their child turns out as anything less than a national leader or a scientist who discovers the cure for cancer or a professional sports star, they must have failed. Others, perhaps half jokingly, state their aims as too low. "If they get out of high school without getting arrested, I've done my job."

Practicing the priority of love is built on the simple foundation of choice, goals, and time. Yesterday we reinforced the truth that priorities begin with our choice. Today we look at the fact that unless we set goals based on the priorities we've chosen, we'll end up constantly frustrated by the feeling that we're not doing what we want in our parenting.

To get to what we are aiming for as parents, a great place to start is the example of Jesus as he grew up: "Jesus kept increasing in wisdom and stature, and in favor with God and men" (Luke 2:52 NASB). We're aiming for growth in four areas of life reflected in this verse: intellectual (wisdom), physical (stature), spiritual (favor with God), and social (favor with men).

**intellectual:** to encourage and support your child's education

**physical:** to protect and nurture your child physically

**spiritual:** to guide your child to a strong personal relationship with God

**social:** to pass on to your child life skills to live responsibly as an independent adult

If you can help your child grow in those four ways, you can consider yourself successful as a parent. They can grow in these ways regardless of any circumstances they face, despite any mistakes they make or setbacks they have, and free from any comparisons with others. The goal of parenting is not some false image of foolproof success we or others may build up for our children. Instead, it is the privilege of living life in the direction of the growth only God can cause in their lives.

These goals can be seemingly small but still extremely significant. It could be a goal to read a book or to start eating breakfast together or to get them to play outside with you each day. A popular book talks about BHAGs for business goals — calling them Big Hairy Audacious Goals.* While this is a great strategy for corporations, I believe in LHAGs for families — Little Happy Achievable Goals. Start there and build together!

It's important to remember that goals are not guarantees. There are no guarantees in parenting. Think back

---

*Jim Collins and Jerry I. Porras, *Built to Last: Successful Habits of Visionary Companies* (New York: HarperBusiness, 2004), 91.

to how it was for a couple held captive in ancient Egypt. Jochebed looked into the big brown eyes of her son and thought about the uncertainties of being a parent. They had started while she was still pregnant. The usual wondering about whether a boy or a girl was on the way was deeply and desperately amplified by the oppression of the Egyptians. Fearful the Israelite slaves were growing too large and powerful as a nation, the Egyptians had begun to kill any newborn baby boy, allowing only the girls to live. Think of the range of emotions Jochebed and her husband, Amram, experienced as the birth approached. Anticipation mixed with terror. Hope mixed with fear.

Their baby was born—and it was a boy. At certain risk to their own lives, they decided to hide the boy from the Egyptian murderers. They named him Moses.

Amram and Jochebed sailed full speed into the storm of uncertainty that is called parenting. Knowing they could not hide the baby Moses for long, a trembling Jochebed found herself at the Nile River, placing her baby into a straw basket. The daughter of Pharaoh was just down the river. If only Jochebed could float Moses in front of her eyes, perhaps this princess of Egypt would feel love for this baby and spare his life.

With courageous love, Jochebed released her baby to the uncertain currents of the Nile, toward an unknown destination, uncertain of how the daughter of Pharaoh would respond, unsure of what any of this would mean for the future or whether she would ever see her baby again. What a picture of what it means to be a parent! (From Exodus 1–2.)

• • •

Parenting is planned uncertainty! Goals do not remove the uncertainty of life; they just give us direction in the midst of it all. Jochebed wasn't sure how Pharaoh's daughter would respond, and yet she planned for the best response. She sent her daughter, Miriam, to be nearby when the daughter of Pharaoh took the baby from the basket. Jochebed prompted Miriam to suggest that there was a Jewish woman who would be willing to care for this new baby if the pharaoh's daughter were to choose to take him into Pharaoh's house. The daughter agreed, and Moses of the household of Pharaoh was raised by his mother Jochebed.

There is something about Jochebed's launching of that little baby in a basket that is profound for us as parents. She was releasing him toward the highest potential for life and growth. This is exactly what we do over and over again. It doesn't start when our children drive off to college; it starts when they begin to crawl down the hall. We live the balancing act of keeping them as safe as possible while releasing them in the sometimes dangerous direction of growth. What a challenge! It's a deep reminder of our desperate need to trust in God.

As you set goals in parenting, it's vital to remember that healthy goals are statements of faith and not attempts to control. Our goals should grow out of our faith. Do you want to see the great capacity for faith that human beings possess? Just watch parents view an ultrasound of their not-yet-born baby. They study a video screen filled with confusing electronic snow; yet based on the word of a technician, Mom and Dad ooh and aah over their baby's cute little turned-up nose. They rejoice in the announcement that "it's a boy" or "it's a girl"; and to prove their faith, they go home and paint the nursery blue or pink.

God sees our hearts and lives more clearly than any ultrasound ever could. He not only knows our now; he knows our future. When he speaks to us about our children and our parenting, we can trust what he tells us and act on this trust.

This desire to trust God as we set goals and make plans for our family is often tested by the realities of life. As a sort of parable of the emotions we face as parents who are seeking to trust, I recall a trip to a beach while on a family vacation. Our older two, in their teen years, were playing in the surf while Chaundel and I played on the sand with our youngest. The water at this beach was so shallow that they were able to walk in water no higher than their waist out to a rock a hundred yards or so out, where they sat and talked for a time. As they talked, the tide came in quickly. Chaundel and I, standing on the shore, saw them get off the rock and try to walk back in, but the water was now up to their chins. They tried to swim, but we could see them struggling with a current that was too strong to swim against. They went back to hang on to the rock.

I had just read a news story about a family being lost to an ocean current after a boat capsized, so I began to feel a sense of panic. Here were our children, only a hundred yards away, and I didn't have the power to help them without getting caught up in the same currents they were battling. I felt helpless.

Just as we began to look up the beach for a lifeguard station, a man in a kayak noticed our children's plight. He paddled over to them and had them grab on to the kayak. With great effort that showed how strong the currents were, he made his way back to the shore. He dropped them off about twenty-five yards out, and we waved our great appreciation.

Our children were now safe, but later I began to let worry get to me. What if that man hadn't shown up? What if we hadn't been able to find a lifeguard? What if our kids had tried to swim but then got caught in a current that took them out to sea? First I had felt helpless because of what could happen, and now I was feeling anxious about what might have happened!

The truth behind our trust is that God is with us in every circumstance of life. He was with us on the beach, with our children on the rock, and with the man in the kayak. The depth of our trust is that God would be with us—with a promise of eternity and a presence of comfort—even in the face of some tragedy. God is the perfect parent, and he offers to give you the strength and wisdom you need to parent. Philippians 4:13 reads, "I can do everything through him who gives me strength." Think about this verse in relationship to parenting. James 1:5 (NLT) reads, "If you need wisdom—if you want to know what God wants you to do—ask him, and he will gladly tell you. He will not resent your asking." God loves you and he loves your kids, and he wants to give you the wisdom you need.

God's strength and wisdom come into our lives as parents as we trust in him. So here is the big question: How exactly does this work? If you've found yourself asking for strength yet still feeling weak, asking for wisdom but feeling you hear no answer, you certainly are not alone. In fact, this is a more common experience than feeling some supernatural burst of energy or seeing God's wisdom written across the sky. God obviously could give us wisdom and strength in these ways, but he more often gives them in the midst of the moment as we take each step of faith. I've often asked myself why God does it this way. My conclusion is that it causes us to remember to trust personally in God, who gives the strength, rather than just looking for strength as though it is some product God impersonally dispenses. Parenting is a relationship, and the strength and wisdom we need for parenting come from a relationship —a relationship with God that provides what we need as we need it.

As we look at the priority of parenting this week, we are reminded that our priorities begin with our choice and then must be expressed in our goals. Set Little Happy Achievable Goals; set these goals knowing they are not guarantees; and establish your goals with a deepening sense of trust in God.

### Response from the Heart of a Mom

*I become easily overwhelmed in thinking about everything I need to teach my children. I can't keep it all straight! And there are many things I'm just not qualified to teach them. Boiling it down to Luke 2:52 helps, but the key for me has always been this: The most important thing to teach my kids is to have their own relationship with God and to trust him with their lives. And it all circles back to my own need to learn how to trust him myself—especially in this area of parenting.*

WEEK 1, DAY 3: **Priorities Are Expressed in My Goals**

- **Verse to remember:** "Jesus kept increasing in wisdom and stature, and in favor with God and men" (Luke 2:52 NASB).

- **Action to take:** Ask God for wisdom right now in some specific decision or direction for your parenting.

- **Tomorrow:** Priorities are done in my time.

# Priorities Are Done in My Time

Love is spelled out in our daily lives with four letters: T-I-M-E. Jesus taught that nothing is more important than relationships. Unless you spend time with someone, you don't really have a relationship with them. I invite you to pray with me this prayer from the book of Psalms as we begin today's reading: "Teach us to make the most of our time, so that we may grow in wisdom" (Psalm 90:12 NLT).

There is a familiar tug-of-war between "quality time" and "quantity time." Some say that the quantity of time you spend with your kids is most important; others believe that the quality of time is what really counts. The truth is, *both are important*. Who said we have to choose between these two? They are certainly not mutually exclusive. Do you want to go to a restaurant that serves a big steak or a delicious steak? You want both! When you go fishing, do you want to catch the largest fish or the most fish? Both! Do your children most need quality time or quantity time? They need both intensely focused attention and hours of sheer availability and presence.

Spending time with your kids doesn't happen automatically; it has to be planned. During the first three days of our thirty-day journey together (you're already 10 percent through the study), we talked about the priority of love in your parenting. We've been reminded that parenting is a priority, that nothing becomes a priority until we make it a priority, and that our goals determine the direction our priorities take us.

Think of today's reading more as a practical worksheet than a set of new ideas. As you love your kids with your time, here are four specific things you can do:

## 1. Schedule dates.

Things move up the list of priorities when we do three things: *plan* them, *schedule* them, and *do* them. It all starts with planning. What could you plan to do to make a bad relationship better? Even more important, what could you plan to do to make a good relationship great? Then you take the time to put it on the calendar, a simple step that if ignored is the downfall of many of us. Then you do it.

A date is anything you write on your calendar. Many of the best dates with your children are already there—birthdays, Christmas, Easter, and maybe a yearly family reunion. Since you know you're going to celebrate those dates, put some things into motion on those days that help you more strongly connect as a family. The key point is this: make a relational connection a part of the date. On your child's birthday, this could mean a time of affirming their gifts at breakfast. When they're younger, you could put one chocolate chip in their pancake for every affirmation—just to add some fun. At Christmas, our family has always celebrated a "birthday party for Jesus." We have a birthday cake for Jesus and blow out a candle; but even more significantly, we take a moment to talk about the gift we want to give Jesus during the next year and what we're thankful for in the last year. On your family vacation, you might read inspiring books or practice Scripture memorization together if you're on a long car ride.

As important as birthdays and holidays are, the other times we schedule to be with our children may end up being the most meaningful. Such occasions can be anything from a playdate with a friend at the park when they are in preschool to a two-week mission trip together during the high school years. Perhaps you could do what *you* want half of the time and what *they* want the other half. As much as you may want your children to go to the nearby museum or cultural center, it may not be the date of their dreams. Some awesome things happen in your child's development when you ask them what they want to do and build a date around that desire. Also, it just may be a lot of fun!

## 2. Establish routines.

We are all creatures of habit, and in the end the contribution of our lives will have been determined much more by the habits we kept than by any single moment or event. We intuitively know the truth of seventeenth-century English poet John Dryden's statement, "We first make our habits, and then our habits make us." The encouragement in these words is this: we have the opportunity to make our habits. When you feel you are not spending the time you would like with your children, make a new habit.

These routines are often built around bedtime. Reading a brief story and praying together before they go to sleep have an enduring power in your child's life. When they are in preschool, the scintillating reading may be, "See the cat's eyes, see the cat's nose, see the cat's toes, now watch the cat doze." I'm sure you've noticed almost all books for pre-schoolers end with someone or something going to sleep — in the hope that the power of suggestion will put your child to sleep as you read. I've often thought that publishers of children's books might be tempted to have the Bible end with the words "God created the new heavens and earth, and they all took a nap!" As your children get older, perhaps you could read a chapter a night from a series like Little House on the Prairie or the Chronicles of Narnia. Bedtime is also one of the best times to get your children to talk with you. When they walk in the door from school, they may just give you a quick "fine" in answer to your question about how their day went. At bedtime, they'll talk on and on because they think they are getting away with staying up a little later.

There are many other times to establish routines — a snack when your kids get home from school or a connection in the morning around the breakfast table. I know some families who ask, "What were the highs and lows of your day?" around the dinner table. As you establish these habits, think carefully about the routines you are building with regard to the technologies and entertainments in our lives. Too often we find ourselves going in entirely different directions — one to play a video game, another to watch TV, another to spend time on a social networking site. The solutions to these barriers that technology can build between us are as varied as our families and personalities. You could choose to play video games with your kids on occasion or proclaim one night a week a technology-free night or have only one TV in your home so that all programs are watched together. Whatever solution you choose, the idea is to use technology as an additional tool to build relationships.

## 3. Love as you go.

Here's a radical thought: All of the time you spend with your children does not have to be time you give to them; some of it should be time they give to you. As you go on an errand, they go with you (as they get older, they'll even be able to help you carry something). Sometimes you will barely say a word to each other on the way, but every once in a while, a great conversation will break out. This does not always happen as spontaneously as we would like. Develop a set of questions you can use to draw them out, to help prompt them to talk about not just what they are doing but also what they are feeling. Questions about their interests are a great place to start: What did you do on the playground today? Did you see your friends at lunch? How is that science project going?

One great enemy of these conversations, of course, is the cell phone. If we're not careful, the one memory our children will have of being in the car is seeing us talking on our headset to someone else. On the other hand, the same cell phone can become your best friend in parenting as your children get older. There is something about being involved in one another's lives "as we go"—throughout the day—that keeps the relational connection strong. A quick call or a text can make all the difference for staying in contact. With a daughter living in Rwanda these last three years, one of our favorite connectors has been "Skype To Go." For a small fee, we can call her cell phone throughout the day instead of having to wait until we're both in front of a computer. These are the kinds of connections that keep relationships strong.

## 4. Just do nothing.

Though I have great respect for Nike's famous slogan Just Do It, there are times when it can be healthy to "just do nothing" together. No expectations of conversations, no specific plans, no anticipated outcomes; just sitting together in the same room reading or watching a movie or listening to music—or all three at once. I wish someone would do a study of how Pareto's 80/20 principle applies to our relationships. The principle in the work world is that 20 percent of the work results in 80 percent of the results. I have a sneaking suspicion the same is true of our conversations: 20 percent of the talk results in 80 percent of the meaningful communication. Here's the point: we would choose to have *every* conversation be a great conversation, but life doesn't work that way. It takes the other 80 percent to open the door to a great talk. There is something about just hanging out together, about laughing about something no one else would think is funny, that clears the way for significant conversations. Sometimes the greatest thing you can do with your child as a parent is nothing, as long as you're doing it together.

As you choose to spend time with your children by scheduling dates, establishing routines, loving as you go, and just doing nothing, you are choosing to make love the priority in the most practical and real way—the way you spend your time. The struggle comes in the reality that our time and schedules rarely work out like we want them to, so at times we feel like giving up on planning anything ever again. Hang in there; don't give up! Nothing worthwhile ever happens without some measure of difficulty. Even though it may be a struggle, you end up spending more time and better time with your children than you would have spent otherwise.

### Response from the Heart of a Mom

*I once came home from a women's retreat without any small gift or treat for the kids. Instead, I told them I would give each of them an hour of my undivided attention to be spent in the way they most wanted. They were thrilled! (Granted, they were probably five, nine, and twelve at the time.) One chose to take a piano lesson from me, another to watch a movie together, and another to just hang out in their bedroom and help clean it up a little. I'm pretty good at the "as you go" times, but I know I need to schedule defined intentional times with my kids or they just don't happen.*

WEEK 1, DAY 4: **Priorities Are Done in My Time**

- **Verse to remember:** "Teach us to make the most of our time, so that we may grow in wisdom" (Psalm 90:12 NLT).

- **Action to take:** Try something new in one of the four ways of spending time with your kids that we talked about today.

- **Tomorrow:** Motivated by love

# Motivated by Love

Congratulations! You've already made it to the end of the first week. We've given our attention this week to the priority of love and have been reminded that nothing becomes a priority unless we make it a priority, that our priorities are expressed in our goals, and that they are lived out in the way that we spend our time. Today we turn our focus back to the supreme importance of love. How important is love?

If I speak to my children with the patience of a saint and the wisdom of a prophet, but do not have love, I am only a loud toy drum. If I guide my children to the right education and future, but do not have love, it will all go up in smoke. If I sacrifice my financial future for my children, but do not have love, I give them nothing at all.

You may recognize this as *a parent's paraphrase* of the first few verses of 1 Corinthians 13, the famous "love chapter" of the Bible:

If I speak in the tongues of men and of angels, but have not love, I am only a resounding gong or a clanging cymbal. If I have the gift of prophecy and can fathom all mysteries and all knowledge, and if I have a faith that can move mountains, but have not love, I am nothing. If I give all I possess to the poor and surrender my body to the flames, but have not love, I gain nothing.

1 CORINTHIANS 13:1–3

These verses remind us that even in doing the most important things in life, if there is no love, there is nothing.

None of us love our children as well as we want, so I can already see some of us lining up to buy tickets for a guilt trip as we talk about this, but that's not the purpose of Paul's challenge to love in 1 Corinthians 13; the purpose is to help us live for what is really important. Are you doing what you do for your children out of a motivation of love? "Yes," you say, "but if I'm honest, there is probably more than a little motivation of guilt and pride as well." This is where we all live, so we work on turning up the motivation of love and turning down the pride.

When looking at such powerful truths from God, I'm reminded that others have faced this same battle for millennia. Augustine, speaking in the fourth century of God's emphasis on love over all other gifts in 1 Corinthians 13, said, "All these things are magnificent and from God, but only if they are set upon the foundation of love and rise from the root of love."* Love is the foundation and the root—what great pictures! Without a strong foundation, it doesn't matter how beautiful a building looks on the outside; it will eventually crumble. If a plant's root is cut off, it doesn't matter how much you water and fertilize it; it will certainly shrivel. Without love, it doesn't matter how great

---

*Quoted in Judith L. Kovacs, *1 Corinthians* (Grand Rapids: Eerdmans, 2005), 217.

your parenting technique is or how many sacrifices you make; your efforts will eventually fall short.

Augustine also reminds us of why the priority of love is so vital: "Unless our will is good, we cannot use anything well. And when love is absent, the will cannot be good."* Apart from love, I must find some other primary motivation to keep me doing what I'm doing. Honestly, I'm all for getting yourself through a tough day by looking forward to a scoop from the ice cream carton in the back of your freezer—behind the peas and carrots where your kids would never dare look! However, without love, these secondary motivations must move into first place. So you find yourself using guilt, shame, pride, reward, anxiety, fear, or mere duty as the main motivation in your relationship with your children.

A secondary motivation that all too easily slips into first place is our tendency to keep score as parents. We get set up from the moment our child is born. The very first thing they are given is an Apgar score! While the Apgar actually provides a good picture of our child's health, I wish we didn't call it a score. In a competitive society, we find ourselves comparing the head size and weight of our babies and then the age at which they walk and talk. It's almost impossible not to compare; the danger comes when the comparison turns into a mental score and the score becomes a motivator for our parenting. Maybe you don't have a competitive bone in your body and so don't need protection from this temptation; for most of us, however, memorizing a verse like Galatians 5:6 can be a transforming experience for our parenting. "The only thing that counts is faith expressing

---

*Ibid., 218.

itself through love." No comparison there! Instead, there is the freedom of the simple decision to trust in God and to express your love for your children out of this trust.

In all our talk about the priority of love, a question must be asked: Do you tell your children you love them? "They know," you say. "They can see it in what I do." Let them hear it too! Dads, one of the greatest protections from harm you will ever give your children is in the words "I love you." These words can protect them from getting caught up in circumstances or from chasing after relationships that could hurt them the rest of their lives. It is tragic that we sometimes protect our children from the harm of a cruel world, only to do them a greater cruelty by not letting them know we love them. Why, then, is saying "I love you" so difficult for some people? Because we have to set aside our fear, our pride, or our past in order to say it. These words are never spoken out of anxiety, fear, or pride. If you had a parent who never said they loved you, it wasn't because of you; it was because of their own issues with anxiety, fear, or pride. The words "I love you" are spoken out of the priority of love—God's love for you expressed to the children he has given you to love.

I can think of no better way to end this week of talking about the priority of love than by focusing on the priority of *God's love for you*. Make it your intention this week—and every week—to do whatever best allows your heart to hear the love God has for you as his child. Maybe it's listening to Christian music, stopping long enough to hear God's voice in the words. Maybe it's taking a quiet walk, experiencing the grandeur of our Creator. Maybe it's meditating on Scriptures that speak of God's love for you (look for the list in day 2 of next week's reading). Maybe it's in having a running conversation with God throughout the events of your day. Nothing is more foundational to loving your children than taking the time to know that you are loved.

### Response from the Heart of a Mom

*I am appalled when I take a step back and truly look at the motivations of my parenting sometimes. Genuine love appears nowhere to be found. Too often I show "love" to my children because it is in my best interest. It meets my own needs to feel loving, seem successful, or get my to-do list done. Exposing the wrong motivation for what I do for my kids and looking for love are essential for me. The only way I've found to truly make love a priority in my parenting is to make sure, as Tom reminded us, that I'm basking in God's unconditional love and acceptance of me. Actually, every one of his suggestions has worked for me at one time or another to bring to mind God's love for me.*

WEEK 1, DAY 5: **Motivated by Love**

- **Verse to remember:** "The only thing that counts is faith expressing itself through love" (Galatians 5:6).

- **Action to take:** Tell your children today that you love them.

- **Next week:** Parenting Principle #2: Love with new power.

# Love with New Power

## The Power of Your Love

We love each other as a result of his loving us first.

1 John 4:19 NLT

# Finding
# a New Pattern

The action of loving our children the way Jesus loves us reminds me of the humorous story of two brothers. A mom was preparing pancakes for her sons, Kevin, five, and Mikey, three. The boys began to argue over who would get the first pancake. Their mother saw the opportunity for a lesson on love. "If Jesus were sitting here, he would say, 'Let my brother have the first pancake; I can wait." Kevin turned to his younger brother and said, "Mikey, you be Jesus."

How does the challenge to you as a parent to love like Jesus make you feel? Many parents I've talked to respond with the words "frustrated, inadequate, tired." This challenge can cause you to think, "Is nothing ever enough? I've been encouraged to spend more time with my kids, and I'm working on that. Then I actually pick up a book to read about loving my children. I should get some credit for that. Now I'm told my standard for love is no less than *Jesus*. How am I ever going to get there?"

If the challenge seems impossible, I'm right there with you. Yet there is hope! God can do what we cannot. John, one of Jesus' disciples, is the one who recorded Jesus' command for us: "Love one another. As I have loved you, so you must love one another" (John 13:34). Toward the end of his life, this same John wrote, "This is love for God: to obey his commands. And his commands are not burdensome" (1 John 5:3). *Not burdensome!* To follow the command to love like Jesus, John said, is not burdensome. What had he discovered? And how can I incorporate this discovery into the way I love? This is the journey we're going to embark on this week—the journey toward *greater love with less burden*.

We begin with this question: How do we love like Jesus? If we're to love everyone as Jesus loved, this must include the people who are closest to us. For this to happen, we need four things that are promised in Jesus' command to love: a better example, a stronger foundation, a higher purpose, and a greater power. We'll look this week at the awesome love that comes from these four gifts, beginning with the first today.

In order to love as Jesus loved, we need *a better example*. Jesus urges us to love one another "as I have loved you." He is the example, the model of love. This ideal example of love is important to the extreme in your parenting. To be a good parent, you must understand the power of example. In relationships, all of us tend to follow the examples that have been set for us.

We tend to have the kind of marriage our parents had. We don't have to, but we tend to. If all things are left to themselves, without extra attention given, we will tend to drift toward what we know, the example we had growing up. If you grew up in a home where your parents displayed affection for each other openly, you'll tend to do the same; if you grew up in a home where a hug was a rare event, this is the way you'll naturally drift. The excitement, of course, comes when our backgrounds are entirely different! In marriage, opposites attract and then opposites attack. The open displays of affection that attracted you to your spouse because they were so different from what you grew up with may well irritate you in your new marriage because they don't fit the picture you are used to experiencing. You may not even know why the irritation is there, but it is. It is extremely difficult to break the power of the example that has been set for us.

This principle has deep implications for our parenting. As parents, we tend to raise our children as we were raised. If you grew up in a loud home, with everyone talking at once, this is the way your family will drift. If you grew up in a home where it was so quiet that a single fly buzzing in the window brought a four-alarm response, this is the way you'll naturally bend. One way isn't right and another wrong; it's just two different family cultures. If you've ever heard or seen your parents in the words you use and actions you take, you understand the power of example.

Here's the big question: What if we've been given some bad examples to follow? In one sense it's not a question at all. None of us had perfect parents, and so there are bad examples in even the best of parents. For many of us it goes deeper than this. You want to be a great parent, yet you realize the example your parents set was terribly broken. Maybe your parents abandoned you or rarely spent time with you. Maybe they deeply hurt you.

So we want to change, and we try to change. We may

even successfully make a change, but at great cost. We're worn-out inside, wondering if we can keep it up for a few more months or years. I know many couples who gave their all in raising their kids, to the extent that when the kids left home, they were so worn-out they had nothing left to give to each other. I do *not* want this to happen to you. There has to be a better plan.

It's not enough to just want to break a bad pattern. In order to change the way you love, you must find a *new* pattern.

Jesus gave us a new commandment because a new commitment is not enough. The magnet of the models you've been given keeps pulling you back. The more you say, "I'm not going to be like them," the more you focus on the old model, and the stronger the magnetic pull becomes! The harder you try, the more difficult it seems to be, and the more tired you get.

You need a new and stronger magnet! That is what Jesus offers in his new commandment. The example of Jesus, lived out in daily relationship with him, can give you strength to live in new ways. The old magnet of past patterns has not vanished; instead, you have a new and greater power drawing you in a new direction. Have you been trying harder until you're tired of trying? If there is any one gift we could give you through the reading of this book, it would be the freedom to stop trying and start trusting, to stop trying to love your kids better and start trusting Jesus for a refreshing strength to love your children greater. This will be our focus this week.

## Response from the Heart of a Mom

*I am so grateful for the amazing examples I had in the love shown to me throughout my life. I experienced unconditional, consistent, sacrificial love from my parents. Sure, they made a lot of mistakes with their kids, even obvious ones, but not in the area of loving us. We knew we could count on their love, no matter what we did or said or felt. They never withheld their love.*

*Their great example could actually discourage me even more as a parent. I can easily accept that I can't love my kids as unconditionally as Jesus does, but I have often felt I can't even love them as sacrificially as my parents loved me. At times I want to give up because the task seems too daunting. But this is exactly where God wants me—desperate to the point of realizing that the huge task of loving my children the way he wants them to be loved is impossible on my own. It is only as I turn to him and experience the limitless source of unconditional love in my own life that I am able to love my children the way he planned for them to be loved.*

*No matter how precious that tiny baby is, how sweet that adorable four-year-old is on a good day, or how impressive it is when your teen decides to clean their room without being asked—even in those moments when you think you couldn't love your children more —the emotion of love that wells up in your heart is not enough. It won't last. It is conditioned on your child's good behavior, on them remembering all the wise training you've given them, on their God-given cuteness. The kind of deep, abiding love necessary for the long haul of parenting is found only in immersing yourself in the deep, deep love that Jesus has for you.*

WEEK 2, DAY 6: **Finding a New Pattern**

- **Verse to remember:** "Love one another. As I have loved you, so you must love one another" (John 13:34).

- **Action to take:** Pray that Jesus' model of love will give you new patterns for your parenting.

- **Tomorrow:** Getting the right foundation

# Getting the Right Foundation

To love your kids the way Jesus loves you, you not only need the better example we talked about yesterday; you also need *a stronger foundation*. An example shows us the direction to go, but it is in our foundation of love that we find the strength to go in that direction. We talked yesterday about the challenge to love like Jesus. For this kind of love, don't miss Jesus' foundational words in his new commandment: "I have loved you." We need the foundation of his love in order to love our children the way Jesus loves us.

Each of us has tried to make another person's love the foundation for our love for others—maybe a parent, friend, or spouse. But what happens when we don't feel their love? We can get trapped in the downward spiral of "you don't feel like loving me, so I won't feel like loving you," and then it becomes abundantly clear that we need a stronger foundation. We need a love that will never fail us.

Jesus loves you just like that. Jesus laid down his life for you! The most eternally significant moment in your life comes when you first recognize the truth, "Jesus loves me."

You cannot give what you have not received. You cannot

give unconditional love unless you have received unconditional love. You cannot give unselfish love unless you have
received unselfish love. You cannot give patient love unless
you have received patient love. You cannot love in forgiveness unless you have been loved in forgiveness.

I've talked to many people who know that God loves
them, but they don't really feel his love. We're rightly taught
that you cannot feel your way into a faith in God and that
faith is not about a certain way of feeling. While it is true
that faith is not found in a feeling, it is also true that faith
is not without feelings. Emotions are not the proof of your
faith, yet they should be the result of your faith. How could
you not feel *something* about the amazing truth that God
loves you?

How would you describe the way God's love feels to you?
To some it might feel like a warm hug, to others a strong
place of protection, to others a deep sense of peace, to others an exploding sense of joy. I'm not talking about forcing
yourself to feel a certain way. It's more about connecting
personally with God's love.

Find a place where you can focus on this list of verses
from the Bible. As you read, hear God's voice speaking to
your life—maybe as you've never heard it before.

> You are forgiving and good, O Lord, abounding in love
>     to all who call to you. (Psalm 86:5)
>
> Great is your love, reaching to the heavens; your
>     faithfulness reaches to the skies. (Psalm 57:10)
>
> How priceless is your unfailing love! Both high and low
>     among men find refuge in the shadow of your wings.
>     (Psalm 36:7)

"With everlasting love I will have compassion on you," says the LORD, your Redeemer. (Isaiah 54:8 NLT)

So now there is no condemnation for those who belong to Christ Jesus. (Romans 8:1 NLT)

I am convinced that neither death nor life, neither angels nor demons, neither the present nor the future, nor any powers, neither height nor depth, nor anything else in all creation, will be able to separate us from the love of God that is in Christ Jesus our Lord. (Romans 8:38–39)

I pray that you, being rooted and established in love, may have power, together with all the saints, to grasp how wide and long and high and deep is the love of Christ. (Ephesians 3:17–18)

The LORD your God is with you, he is mighty to save. He will take great delight in you, he will quiet you with his love, he will rejoice over you with singing. (Zephaniah 3:17)

What marvelous love the Father has extended to us! Just look at it—we're called children of God! (1 John 3:1 MSG)

Because of his great love for us, God, who is rich in mercy, made us alive with Christ even when we were dead in transgressions—it is by grace you have been saved. (Ephesians 2:4–5)

For God so loved the world that he gave his only Son, so that everyone who believes in him will not perish but have eternal life. (John 3:16 NLT)

This is real love. It is not that we loved God, but that he loved us and sent his Son as a sacrifice to take away our sins. (1 John 4:10 NLT)

Jesus said, "I've loved you the way my Father has loved
   me. Make yourselves at home in my love." (John 15:9
   MSG)

Look again at that phrase in the last verse: "at home in
my love." Things are better at home when I'm at home in
God's love.

Ephesians 5:1–2 reads, "Be imitators of God, therefore,
as dearly loved children and live a life of love, just as Christ
loved us and gave himself up for us as a fragrant offering
and sacrifice to God." "As dearly loved children" — one of
the most empowering steps you can take to love your child
is to realize that *you* yourself are a dearly loved child. Never
get over that! Want to be a great parent? Feel, really feel,
how deeply God loves you!

The love God has for you is powerfully pictured in the
experience Abraham faced with his son Isaac. Abraham
lived in a culture that believed the ultimate expression of
trust in a god was to sacrifice your child to that god. As we
enter this story, the true God is about to teach Abraham
that he abhors child sacrifice and that he instead asks for a
sacrifice of the heart. Abraham is about to learn an amazing lesson about trust and love.

Think back to how this loving father, Abraham, must
have felt as he walked up the mountain with his son. Each
step up the mountain Abraham could feel the burden of
stress and doubt weighing him down. How could he trust
God with this? Next to him walked Isaac, carrying a load
of wood they would use for a sacrifice when they reached
the top of the mountain. Isaac didn't know that God had
told Abraham to sacrifice *him* on that mountaintop. Before
they had begun their climb, Isaac asked his father why they

weren't taking a lamb for the sacrifice. He heard the strain in his father's voice as he said, "God himself will provide the lamb." Now they walked together in unfamiliar silence. Abraham was struggling with his thoughts. He must have considered the faith journey of his life; the difficult things God had asked him to do. When God asked him to leave his homeland, Abraham said yes. He discovered he could trust God in that move to the Promised Land. God had told Abraham he would have a son, and Abraham had waited twenty-five years to see that he could trust God's word. Isaac had been born, the child of promise.

Now Abraham hears God's voice again. He knows it is God's voice because he has heard it before. This time God asks Abraham to sacrifice Isaac. How can he trust God with this? As he climbs the mountain, Abraham reasons that even in this he can trust. He knew God had promised that his family would become a great nation through Isaac. He knew God had told him to make a sacrifice of Isaac. He had seen again and again that he could trust God. So he reasoned (Hebrews 11) that God must be about to do a miracle of resurrection. Since a nation would come through Isaac, if Isaac should happen to be killed, God would obviously need to resurrect him. Faced with confusion and doubt and darkness, Abraham chooses to trust God.

God has a different plan! Not resurrection, but substitution. He stops Abraham from sacrificing Isaac and instead provides the sacrifice of a ram. In this one act, God shows Abraham he is not a God who asks for child sacrifice, calls him to a sacrifice of the heart, and pictures through Abraham his plan to one day send Jesus as a sacrifice. Why would God put Abraham through this? To foreshadow through Abraham the once-for-all sacrifice that would one day be provided in Jesus. (From Genesis 22.)

• • •

The trust and relief Abraham felt that day can be the experience of every parent. God provides the sacrifice. God would not allow the sacrifice of Abraham's son Isaac, yet God himself chose the sacrifice of his only Son, Jesus. "For God so loved the world that he gave his one and only Son, that whoever believes in him shall not perish but have eternal life" (John 3:16).

The foundation for a deeper love for others is found in the depth of God's love for you. Pray a grateful prayer: "Father, thank you for your love and sacrifice for me. I want to live in relationship to you, trusting in the gift of forgiveness and life that comes through Jesus."

### Response from the Heart of a Mom

*On those days when I realize that the reservoir of love I need to be able to truly love our children seems to have run dry, I can run to the truth that God really does love me unconditionally. Every one of the verses Tom listed speaks to me, so if I will just stop for five minutes, realize my emptiness, and read even a few of these verses, I can be refreshed in God's love for me. As I look at the sacrifice of Jesus on the cross, my love tank is refilled.*

WEEK 2, DAY 7: **Getting the Right Foundation**

- **Verse to remember:** "For I am convinced that neither death nor life, neither angels nor demons, neither the present nor the future, nor any powers, neither height nor depth, nor anything else in all creation, will be able to separate us from the love of God that is in Christ Jesus our Lord" (Romans 8:38–39).

- **Action to take:** Write out some of your favorites from the list of verses expressing God's love for us and put them on your refrigerator or some other place where you will see them regularly throughout the day.

- **Tomorrow:** Discovering a higher purpose

# Discovering
# a Higher Purpose

In most love songs and romantic movies, love is the highest purpose. If you can find that one great love, you have fulfilled your destiny, discovered your meaning, and reached the stars!

This is certainly not real life. Real life is asking yourself, "What happens after the end of the movie, the last note of the song?" Does the couple stare affectionately into each other's eyes for the next forty years? Of course not. They would grow bored with each other and descend into petty irritation within weeks, if not days, if that was all there was to their relationship. Love, even the greatest love, must have a purpose higher than itself.

As we think about loving our kids the way Jesus loves us, we have looked the last two days at the truths that we need the better model of his love and the stronger foundation of knowing we are loved by him. Today, we remind ourselves that we also need *a higher purpose* than just our own love. Jesus teaches clearly that love is to be our highest priority —love for God and love for others. But this highest priority has an even higher purpose. If love's highest purpose is itself, it will end up caving in on itself. The higher purpose Jesus points to in his new command is this: to let the world see *whose we are*. "By this all men will know that you are my disciples, if you love one another" (John 13:35). Our love for one another, Jesus says, will be the greatest evidence to those around us that we are his followers.

This means the highest purpose of parenting is not to have a "good family," a "loving family," or a "fun family"; the highest purpose is to help our children know and glorify God—to show the world the heart of God through the way we live our lives. I know some will think, "Well, our family doesn't fit this picture. We can't even be a good family—how are we going to be a God-glorifying family?"

God loves to glorify himself, even through families that struggle their way to faith. Think about the struggles of one of the Bible's most famous families—Jacob's family. In all of history there may never have been a father who set up his son for failure like Jacob. He should have known better. He had seen in his own childhood what the seeds of sibling rivalry can grow into. Jacob had fought with his brother, Esau, for parental approval—with disastrous results. Now Jacob is trying to give his youngest son, Joseph, the love he had never received as the youngest son from his father, Isaac. Because of his pain, Jacob overcompensates as a father and shows a special love for Joseph while ignoring Joseph's ten older brothers.

The older brothers' emotional reaction is predictable; they hate their little brother. Joseph doesn't help matters; he treats his brothers with juvenile pride. While the response of these brothers is predictable, the action they take is shocking. While working out in the fields, they plot to kill him, but one of the brothers convinces the others to throw Joseph into a deep hole. Seeing a caravan of foreigners traveling by, they decide to make a little money and alleviate some guilt by selling their own brother into slavery.

Where is their father, Jacob, during all of this? He may have been at home, yet he is right in the middle of this story. He may have thought it was love; yet in his reaction to the pain of his own childhood, Jacob not only sets the stage; he writes the script for all that played out that day between these brothers. With one son sold into slavery and the other sons lying about what had happened, Jacob's failures as a father are on open display for all to see.

It's tempting to think, "Failure as a father; end of story." But God is not finished with Jacob as a parent. In fact, to our total amazement, God is going to birth an entire nation out of this mess of a family life. Jacob's twelve sons will become the twelve tribes of Israel. As flawed as Jacob is as a father, he continues to love his children. You can see his love in the way he grieves for his lost son. You can see it even in his still-flawed overprotection of Benjamin, a younger son born after Joseph disappeared. In Jacob's family, mistakes are made, sins are committed, guilt is hidden, and love is still chosen.

Years later, God will bring this family back together again, with Joseph now a leader in Egypt. The older brothers are given an opportunity to deal with their guilt and suspicions. Joseph shows he has worked through his bitterness when he says to his brothers, "You meant it for evil, but God meant it for good." Jacob is then restored to a place of honor as the father of a family that has great flaws and great struggles—and is also used in a great way to bless the world. (From Genesis 37–50.)

• • •

There is no such thing as a perfect family. From the outside, some families may look like good families; others may look like struggling families. None are perfect. God can work in and through all families, no matter what they look like to us who observe from outside. The higher purpose of parenting is not to try to look like the good family down the block. The higher purpose is to *glorify God* from this point forward, no matter what your family looks like. Whatever your family has been through, I am certain of this: God wants to use your family to bless the world. This will happen not by presenting a false image of perfection but by showing that God can be trusted and glorified even in the midst of life's struggles.

This truth of love's higher purpose is vital for two reasons. First, it keeps us from becoming so focused on the good for our children that we miss the best for them. If our children are doing well, we need to know there is more. If the entire goal of love is having children who do well and do not have problems, the tendency of parents is to become overprotective. Make no mistake: it is one of our great responsibilities as parents to protect our children; but we've all seen what happens when parents become so afraid that they smother instead of love. On the other hand, there is great joy in releasing our children to live out their potential, regardless of the risk. I cannot help but think of Megan, who has cerebral palsy and lives her life in a wheelchair. I've seen her parents encourage her and join her in taking a risk to go to a party, sing on a stage, get on a horse, or ride a wave, resulting in a burst of joy for both Megan and her parents.

Second, the truth of love's higher purpose opens our eyes to see that God has a plan, no matter what the circumstances. Parents who want to be good parents to their children, the kind of parents who would pick up a book like this, can easily slip into the trap of perfectionism. We so want things to go well for our child that we feel we've failed as parents when our child is devastated by a circumstance or led astray by their own decisions. We consider ourselves a failure as parents because we did not reach our goal.

The goal of love is *glorifying God*. This is a goal you can continue to live for, no matter what. Let's be honest: most of us simply want our kids to be happy—and we want to be happy while raising them. How does this feeling connect with God's desire to show his glory through our lives and families? The seventeenth-century French theologian François Fénelon wrote, "It is true that [God] desires our happiness, but that is neither the chief end of his work, nor an end to be compared with that of His glory. It is for His glory only that He wills our happiness."*

When you enjoy a measure of happiness, God can use it for his glory. When you endure a season of struggle, God can use it for his glory. There is no circumstance you face in which God cannot work to show the world what he is like. Like you, I would rather have the happy circumstance. This desire does not change the truth: *in every circumstance you face, God can work to show the world what he is like.*

---

*François Fénelon, *Spiritual Progress* (New York: M. W. Dodd, 1853; e-text, 1997), 10, www.jesus.org.uk/vault/library/fenelon_progress.pdf (May 4, 2011).

## Response from the Heart of a Mom

*It's hard to focus on the end result — that your parenting brings glory to God — when you are potty training a two-year-old. But this is exactly what we need to do — remember what it's really all about. For me, this happens not so much in the midst of the whirlwind of parenting as in my setting aside quiet times to take a long look at why I'm investing in parenting. The early morning, before the day takes on a life of its own, works best for me because I'm too worn-out at night. These times remind me that the ultimate goal is to bring glory to God, both by what happens in me and by what happens in my children's lives.*

WEEK 2, DAY 8: **Discovering a Higher Purpose**

- **Verse to remember:** "You intended to harm me, but God intended it for good to accomplish what is now being done, the saving of many lives" (Genesis 50:20).

- **Action to take:** Ask God for both the strength to face your circumstances and the wisdom to see that he can take even the worst things you face and use them for good.

- **Tomorrow:** Tapping into a greater power

# Tapping into a Greater Power

God is not working to do something fake and plastic and 1950s in your family; he is working to do something real, something that makes a difference. We can fake and pretend in our power, but it wears us out and never lasts. To love like Jesus, we not only need a better model, stronger foundation, and greater purpose; we need *a greater power* —a power that Jesus is willing to give. "As I have loved you, so you must love one another," he said (John 13:34).

As a parent, I know that talking about the greater responsibility of love can be encouraging on one level but discouraging on another. You think, "My biggest battle is getting my kids out the door to school on time, and you're telling me that now I've got to turn my house into a learning place for love? I'd love to see that, but honestly, all I see in our home is a racetrack through the halls, a fast-food stop in the kitchen, and a garbage dump in the kids' rooms. How is this place going to be a cathedral where my kids walk out with a Bible glow on their faces?"

How do you get to this reality? Love—genuine love —happens right in the middle of the reality of life. You should be amazed at the depth of what you are teaching every single day!

- When you yell at one of your kids in the morning and apologize that night, you're teaching them more about forgiveness than they'll learn in any seminary class.

- When you decide to give up the weekly golf game you really enjoy to help a neighbor in need, you're teaching more about selfless serving than they'll learn in years of Sunday school.

- When you hold a baby in your arms, just to hold her close, you're teaching more about security than can be learned in a shelf full of small group Bible studies.

- When you refuse to bow to the insistent pleas of your teen to let them go to a party you know is the wrong place for them to be, you've taught them more about integrity than they'll learn in any character seminar.

How do you get to this place of greater love for a greater purpose? It involves far more than just knowing you need to get there. You have to battle with your children, but even more significantly, you struggle with yourself. If you're like me, the number one thing you must struggle with is your selfishness. I don't *want* to apologize; I want to find a way to get on the golf course. I don't want to take the time to hold a child; I have something pressing I need to get done. Where do you find the power to get past your own selfishness and practice the daily choice to love?

Our dilemma reminds me of those amazing stunts you sometimes see on TV. After launching himself off a roof or creating some huge explosion, someone looks into the camera and says with utter sincerity, "Kids, don't try this at home!" About this kind of love, I say to both kids and parents, "Don't try to love like this in your own power!" To love like Jesus, it is obvious you won't find the power in yourself. The best you can do in your own power is to love like—well, *like you*. To love like Jesus, you need his power in your daily life. The apostle John put it simply: "We love because he first loved us" (1 John 4:19). His love leads the way.

This is the kind of love we need for the realities and complexities of daily family life. I know that as a son I need Jesus' power to love my dad. My dad has struggled with mental illness all his life—cycling for years from somewhat better days to times of great disconnection. How do you love someone when you don't understand the world he is struggling in, when he cannot connect with you? The only way is in recognizing Jesus' love for me and then asking him for the strength to pass this love along.

The need for the power of Jesus' love may be obvious when the situation seems bigger than we can handle; yet the need for his love, although not so obvious to us, is just as important when life seems to be manageable. In fact, one of the greatest things you can do as a parent is to pray the prayer, *Jesus, love through me today*, on an otherwise ordinary, regular, possibly even boring day.

I tend to rely on the power of my own love when I think I have life under control, and then hurry to make the 911 emergency call to bring in the power of Jesus' love when things begin to fall apart. I know this is the wrong thing to do. I know my need for Jesus' love is pictured better by the continual refreshment of living water than by an infrequent emergency call. Yet when life seems even a little easier, I tend to become spiritually lazy and rely on myself alone.

Knowing at least some of us have this tendency, this temptation, how do we begin to make the choice to allow Jesus to love through us every day? I've always been drawn to Paul's encouragement and example of living by Jesus' strength, no matter the circumstance:

> I have learned to be content whatever the circumstances. I know what it is to be in need, and I know what it is to have plenty. I have learned the secret of being content in any and every situation, whether well fed or hungry, whether living in plenty or in want. I can do everything through him who gives me strength.
>
> PHILIPPIANS 4:11–13

Today's reading is about how you can draw on the power of Christ's love every day of your life. We often talk about prayer and Bible reading and church attendance as part of the secret to daily connection to Christ. These are, of course, important, but I have found that without the attitude Paul displays in these verses, you will not draw on the power of Jesus' love in every circumstance of life. That attitude is *contentment*.

Without contentment, you'll find yourself becoming bitter about your circumstances — because none of us have continually pleasant circumstances in this world. Depending on your personality, this bitterness can drive you toward self-reliant achievement or self-deprecating discouragement. One of these choices may look better on the outside, but both drive you away from complete reliance on the love of Christ. The greatest danger of discontentment is that it causes you to trust in what *you* can do instead of in what *God* can do.

Paul points to the answer in the verse some of us memorized as children: "I can do everything through Christ who gives me strength." He is not saying in this verse that Jesus makes you a superman or superwoman—able to out-parent other parents without even breaking a sweat. As you read the verses preceding this one, you see Paul is saying he draws on the strength of Christ in *every circumstance* of life because he realizes *Jesus is there and at work* in every circumstance of life. For better or for worse, for richer or for poorer, in sickness and in health—no matter what the circumstance may be—he knows that Christ is there and is at work.

This connection between my contentment and my daily reliance on Jesus for strength has been a new thought for me. It was a whack on the side of the head to see how powerfully my daily trust in Jesus grows out of my attitude of contentment. I've seen that when I am discontent, I am driven to trust in myself. *When I am content, I find myself trusting in God regardless of the circumstance.* Maybe this is a new thought for you also. You may want to print out this sentence and attach it to your refrigerator or mirror.

To be content does not mean I shouldn't pray for the circumstance to change; it does mean that I realize God can work in my life and my family's life no matter what the circumstance.

### Response from the Heart of a Mom

*I love emergencies. I know, no mother should ever say this, but in thinking about why I love them, it's because in these situations it is a no-brainer for me to depend on Jesus' power. On the other hand, on those normal, nothing-special days, I tend to rely in my own power alone. I get through the day sometimes, but the wear and tear on my kids when I live life on my own power is blatantly and painfully obvious through my irritability or the tone of my voice.*

WEEK 2, DAY 9: **Tapping into a Greater Power**

- **Verse to remember:** "I have learned to be content whatever the circumstances. I know what it is to be in need, and I know what it is to have plenty. I have learned the secret of being content in any and every situation, whether well fed or hungry, whether living in plenty or in want. I can do everything through him who gives me strength" (Philippians 4:11–13).

- **Action to take:** Choose the attitude of contentment in your life today by saying to yourself, "God is at work here," in a situation that would normally cause anxious or restless thoughts.

- **Tomorrow:** Becoming a model parent

# Becoming a Model Parent

An awesome miracle begins to happen when we love our kids the way Jesus loves us, asking for his power to love. Not only do we express God's love to our children; we model it for them so that our kids see our love and also begin to show it to others.

Every parent needs to grasp the tremendous power of modeling. We learn best through what is modeled by others. When we rely on Jesus' love to empower our direction and decisions, we become a part of an amazing work of God—the process of modeling true love. First, Jesus followed the *Father's* example; then we are to follow *Jesus'* example; and finally, and amazingly, others begin to follow *our* example and become an example themselves of the love of God!

***Jesus followed the Father's example for us.*** "I am telling you what my Father has shown me" (John 8:38 NCV). Jesus is perfect. He is God, yet he chose to follow the Father's example in order to be a model to us.

***Then we are to follow Jesus' example.*** "I have given

you an example to follow. Do as I have done to you" (John 13:15 NLT).

*Then we become an example of Jesus' love to others.* "Follow my example, as I follow the example of Christ" (1 Corinthians 11:1). "God had mercy on me, so that Christ Jesus could use me as a prime example of his great patience with even the worst sinners. Then others will realize that they, too, can believe in him and receive eternal life" (1 Timothy 1:16 NLT).

*Finally, they also become an example to others.* "You became a model to all the believers in Macedonia and Achaia" (1 Thessalonians 1:7). "Mark out a straight, smooth path for your feet so that those who follow you, though weak and lame, will not fall and hurt themselves but become strong" (Hebrews 12:13 LB).

As we talked about on day two of week one, there are no guarantees in parenting. We've all seen families in which the parents provided a great example of love, yet their children decided to follow the destructive example of their friends instead. Even when this happens, the good example provided by parents is still there in the back of their minds, constantly inviting them to something better. Your children still have a choice, yet *your* model will almost certainly be the most powerful human model in their lives.

Here are four choices you can make that will empower your model beyond what you ever dreamed possible.

## 1. Choose to spend time with your children.

You cannot model what you cannot see. This is true in even as simple a thing as watching TV together. As they see you react to the good and the bad that make their way across the screen, you are modeling something about Jesus' love. As they see how you make choices about what you will watch together, sometimes giving up your own preferences, you are modeling something about Jesus' love. The point is not that having or not having a TV in the home is the secret to parental success; rather, the point is that one of your main jobs as a parent, especially as your children get older, is to recognize the power of what you model in every circumstance.

## 2. Choose to serve others with your children.

As you model life for your children, be sure to model love for those outside of your family. I love what Paul said to the people he had served at Ephesus: "In everything I did, I showed you that by this kind of hard work we must help the weak, remembering the words the Lord Jesus himself said: 'It is more blessed to give than to receive'" (Acts 20:35). Don't miss the word *showed*. He showed them that by hard work we must help the weak—this is what you have an opportunity to show to your kids. Paul showed the Ephesians a living example of the words of Jesus: "It is more blessed to give than to receive." Show *that* to your kids!

We all want our children to know the blessing of giving to others, and the only way they'll get it from us is if *we* show it. To encourage your kids to show love for others, you may need to make the difficult decision to choose one less activity for them so they can do something to serve the weak, so they can give and not just receive. I've talked to a lot of parents who say, "If I had it to do over again, I'd do less *for* our children and more *with* our children." Involving your kids in activities designed for them is good, and it displays your commitment to them. But you also want to model your commitment to love your neighbor, to love the weak, which may mean choosing one activity and not two —playing soccer but not taking gymnastics, for example. One of the keys to having a strong family is to realize that God wants to work not only *in* your family but also *through* your family.

## 3. Choose to keep talking, even when it seems your kids aren't listening.

Your middle schooler may not say a word to you during the meal, but this doesn't mean you aren't modeling some powerful truths to them through the conversation that they act like they're not hearing!

We all know how this conversation goes. As a parent you ask the questions about their day. "How did your classes go? Was everything OK at lunch? How was the day with your friends?" You know the answer that is on the way; you can feel it coming. Their total day, entire life, complete relational world, and whole classroom schedule is summed up in a one-word answer: "Fine." Even when that's all you get, just keep asking. "Fine" is one word more than none, and they know you care. You just may ask on the very day when something life changing happened, something you never would have discovered if you hadn't kept talking.

As your children grow into adolescence, start telling them more about your day as well. They'll roll their eyes, act bored, and text their friends while you're talking, but sharing about your adult world is a way to prepare them for the adult world they are beginning to enter. And every once in a while, shock them by asking their opinion about what you should do. It may open an unexpected door to conversation with them.

## 4. Choose to model your weaknesses.

Your children are going to see your weaknesses whether you choose to be honest about them or not, so why not be honest about them? Something about being honest about our weaknesses draws us into a different conversation with each other. With a seven-year-old, it may take the form of saying, "I can bandage that cut, but I can't heal it. Let's ask Jesus to make you better." To your seventeen-year-old, you may find yourself saying, "It looks like we may need to move to find work, and we're not really sure of God's direction." Because we are weak, there are a million ways to model our weakness—whether speaking a heartfelt prayer for God's help, letting our child see our tears, stopping to ask directions on the road, or admitting when we got it wrong. One of the greatest ways we model our weakness is through a willingness to utter the words "I'm sorry" when we've made a mistake or caused a hurt.

I confess that this is difficult for me every time I do it. It's amazing that a grown man would be nervous about admitting a weakness to a seven-year old   but I am. Even though you may not feel competent and may stumble over your words, choose to model your weakness.

## 5. Choose to release your children all along the way.

The reason to show the way through your example is so that your children will know the way when they are on their own. The goal of releasing them is always before you, and that is never easy. I remember watching our kindergartner Alyssa march bravely down the school hallway to her first class with a bright smile on her face and a bounce in her step. It was hard to release her. Recently this now twenty-two-year-old daughter marched with the same bright smile and bouncy step toward an airport security gate and a year abroad serving in Rwanda, Africa—and it was hard to release her. Just because it is awfully hard doesn't mean that it isn't abundantly right. The reason that you model is to release.

What we do to model life and faith to our children is exactly what Jesus did for his followers. He is *our* model! This is how Jesus did it:

*He spent time with them.* They walked together, ate together, served together, rowed across the lake together, went to parties together. The disciples learned faith by being together with Jesus in the everyday-ness of life.

*He talked to them.* Even though they often seemed to have no clue what he was saying or were so caught up in their petty jealousies that they missed the amazing truths he was sharing, Jesus kept sharing the truth with them. I'm so glad he did. We're still reading and being changed by the truths shared in the conversations with those disciples. I pray that you also would have the experience of hearing your child repeat something years later that you were convinced they didn't hear when first spoken.

*He shared his weaknesses with them.* Jesus told his followers when he was tired and when he was hungry; as they became more mature, he told them of his deep anguish of soul in Gethsemane: "My soul is overwhelmed with sorrow to the point of death" (Mark 14:34).

*He released them all along the way.* From the very beginning, before most of us would have thought his followers were ready, Jesus was sending them out to do ministry on their own. After three years of discipling, they heard these words from him: "As the Father sent me, I now send you" (John 20:21 NCV).

> ### *Response from the Heart of a Mom*
>
> *It's hard for me to conceal much—including my weaknesses. My life is kind of "out there" for my kids. I find it important to look at what I'm modeling for them through my daily life, though. Probably my biggest area of negative modeling is flashing in anger instead of stopping to think and calm down before I express what I'm feeling. I can only say so many times, "Don't do that like I do." Oh, and that releasing part? It's downright hard! It really is a continual process from the moment they are born. And yet watching our children gain independence gives us great joy.*

WEEK 2, DAY 10: **Becoming a Model Parent**

- **Verse to remember:** "I have given you an example to follow. Do as I have done to you" (John 13:15 NLT).

- **Action to take:** Model your weakness to your children today by asking them to pray that God would meet a personal need in your life.

- **Next week:** Parenting Principle #3: Communicate from the heart.

# Communicate from the Heart

## The Power of Your Words

Praises and curses come from the same mouth! My brothers and sisters, this should not happen. Do good and bad water flow from the same spring?

James 3:10–11 NCV

What comes out of the mouth gets its start in the heart.

Matthew 15:18 MSG

# Words Start
# in the Heart

The power of words to influence a child's life is almost beyond measure. Most of us have personal experience of this truth. You still remember something negative said on a playground or in a classroom in grade school, or you still recall the transforming word of encouragement from a teacher. You can still hear the tone of voice in that playground taunt; you can still see the set of the jaw of that encouraging coach. It may have been ten, twenty, thirty years ago—but the memory is still there. This is the lasting power of words in the heart of a child.

If we want to do our best in communicating to our children, we must understand what Jesus had to say about words. Jesus taught us that our words don't slip out accidentally; they come from our hearts. "What comes out of the mouth gets its start in the heart" (Matthew 15:18 MSG). Words start in the heart. Something in me wants to pretend this isn't true, but everything in me knows it *is* true. When my heart is irritated, I speak rudely. When my heart is threatened, I speak harshly. When my heart is loving, I speak graciously.

Our children often end up absorbing the fallout from our negative attitudes. As adults, we tend to protect our words with other adults. My boss fails to appreciate my hard work, but he is not the one who hears my feelings of disappointment. Instead, I let them build up within me, and they come out in words of anger directed at my children.

We sometimes say the most negative things to the people we love the most. When it is our children, they can't even respond. Jesus' words in Matthew 15 give us hope for real change. Consider these three foundations for change in the way we speak to our children:

## 1. Recognize that your words come from your heart.

Until I recognize the source of my words, change will never happen. It's much easier to blame my circumstances or my weariness or other people's faults for the negative words that I speak. Jesus doesn't let me off the hook. He brings me face-to-face with the reality that the source of my words is my own heart: "The things that come out of the mouth come from the heart" (Matthew 15:18). James wrote, "Praises and curses come from the same mouth! My brothers and sisters, this should not happen. Do good and bad water flow from the same spring?" (James 3:10–11 NCV).

My friends who dig wells in areas of the world that have no fresh water tell me they face a dynamic we also face with our words. They'll go to the work of digging a well, only to find the people of the community will not use its water. Instead, they'll continue to walk long distances to get the same water they have always used. They know this water may make them sick, yet they trust it more than the unknown water from the well. In order to change the pattern, a trusted member of the community must step forward to drink the fresh water. This is not as easy as it sounds, because they are asking a person to change a life-long pattern.

We experience this same pattern with words in our families. Even when there is a fresh source available through God's love, we tend to keep returning to old habits of hurtful and negative words. It is difficult to break our patterns of speech—I call it push-button communication. You say something negative, and I respond with cynicism, just as I always have. Your children say something irritating; you respond with a put-down. You may fervently want to say something different, but when the button is pushed, you can't seem to stop yourself. Knowing that your words come from the heart tells you the only possibility of change begins with a *change of heart*. And, as with the community with the newly dug well, the changed pattern of one person holds the promise to lead others to change.

## 2. Ask God to change your heart.

Without a change of heart, you cannot have a change of words. Oh, you may control your tongue for a time; but the negative attitude will eventually leak out into your words.

What we are talking about is *repentance*. We read this word in the Bible and tend to see it as a negative word, but it is not. *Repent* is one of the most beautiful words in Scripture; it means "to turn around," "to have a fresh start." When you repent, you make a spiritual U-turn by trusting God instead of yourself for change. Parents, we need to repent! We need to say to God, "Lord, I'm sorry I spoke in that way to my child. I want to change, and I need your power to change."

The amazing thing about God's process of change is the way it builds on change. My heart changes—and I speak loving words. The loving words I speak then actually cause my heart to further change. Did you know that every time you speak a loving, gracious, kind word, you are taking a step of spiritual growth? Paul writes, "Speaking the truth with love, we will grow up in every way into Christ, who is the head" (Ephesians 4:15 NCV).

## 3. Ask for forgiveness when you say the wrong thing.

We parents often feel a sting when we've said the wrong thing to our kids. So we take them out for ice cream! We're hoping they'll make the connection: ice cream = apology. Why not just apologize—and then go out for ice cream? One of the greatest teaching moments for our children can come after we've said the wrong thing. I'll never forget the lesson I learned as a young youth pastor. John, a deacon in our church, had offered to let us use his van for our student ministry events. I phoned him because an event was coming up, and he responded with irritation that I would ask. After we hung up, as I sat with confused thoughts, John immediately called back. "I'm sorry," he said. "I wasn't irritated at you. I was upset because things at work really fell apart today. Of course you can use the van for the kids." That call from John is what I remember most, even to this day.

If you say to your kids, "I'm sorry," this is what they'll remember. As they get older, if you're able to go a step further and tell them how your words got their start in your heart, you'll have taught them one of the most valuable lessons in life. "I'm not upset at you. I had a tough day at work, and I let it affect my words to you."

We all struggle with our words, and we always will this side of heaven. The issue is whether you are committed to grow in the way you communicate. Are you taking steps to change your heart—the source of your words? There is hope in the struggle as you admit that words come from the heart, choose to ask God to change your heart, and humbly ask for forgiveness when you say the wrong thing. The positive impact on your children will be immeasurable.

### Response from the Heart of a Mom

*I really don't like the verses in the Bible that speak about our words coming from our hearts. It's hard to admit that my words don't just "come from nowhere." But I find a sort of comfort as I realize that everyone deals with this struggle throughout their lives. I find hope for improvement in stopping to think about my words, knowing that God has promised to help me. If I tell him what I am thinking and work it through with him, then he can work on my heart and bring about positive change in the words I speak.*

WEEK 3, DAY 11: **Words Start in the Heart**

- **Verse to remember:** "What comes out of the mouth gets its start in the heart" (Matthew 15:18 MSG).

- **Action to take:** Ask for forgiveness if you've said a wrong word to one of your children.

- **Tomorrow:** What to say when your child is struggling

# What to Say When Your Child Is Struggling

As we focus this week on communication with our children, today I want to put the emphasis on the right kinds of words for particular situations. Our words need to match the circumstances, and when they don't, we feel it. We all know what it's like to hear joyful words when we need someone to grieve with us or to have someone focus on the negative at a time of celebration. I've always loved the picture the book of Proverbs gives of these ill-fitting words. "If you shout a pleasant greeting to a friend too early in the morning, he will count it as a curse!" (Proverbs 27:14 LB). Proverbs also gives wisdom for the positive use of our words: "The right word spoken at the right time is as beautiful as gold apples in a silver bowl" (Proverbs 25:11 NCV).

Today let's consider the power of a word of encouragement when your child is struggling to do the right thing. "You know that we dealt with each of you as a father deals with his own children, encouraging, comforting and urging you to live lives worthy of God" (1 Thessalonians 2:11–12).

We want our words to motivate our children to positive actions, yet when they struggle, we often fall into using strong negative injunctions in order to move them quickly to action. The last thing we want to be accused of is being soft on our kids, of coddling them when we should be pushing them.

The problem is that negative words are never the most powerful way to motivate us to action. Encouragement is of far greater power. A negative word is like a rock in your shoe; it changes the way you walk only as long as it's there, and you want to get rid of it as quickly as you can. An encouraging word is like giving someone new shoes—new energy and renewed strength to run.

Proverbs talks about this life-sapping nature of negativity: "A nagging spouse is like the drip, drip, drip of a leaky faucet" (Proverbs 27:15 MSG). You cannot help but notice negative words—maybe that's why we use them—but everything in you wants to get away from that sound! In an amazing twist, if all we hear are negative words or nagging, it actually tends to reinforce the wrong action. We want to push against the negativity and run in the opposite direction from the irritation.

I am not saying we can never address something that is wrong. When your child brings home a school progress report with an "F" on the page, of course you don't ignore it! You want to bring about change, and Scripture teaches that the best way to bring change is through positive encouragement, not negative criticism. Some think that being positive means you must pretend the negative never happened. Nothing could be further from the truth! Positive words don't ignore negative circumstances; they just deal with them in a positive way. Instead of saying, "You're so lazy; you'll never amount to anything. You have a life of failure staring you in the face," you could say, "Getting this kind of grade is serious, and it shows you what can happen when you don't work hard in school. I know you can do better. Let's talk about some changes you can make so your next progress report will be different." Negative words look to the past; encouraging words look to the future. Negative words place blame; positive words look for solutions. Negative words promote guilt; encouraging words provide grace.

As much as we know how hurtful it can be, we find ourselves slipping too often into negative speech. It's just easier. We hope it will get results more quickly, and it's often the pattern we grew up with. Some of the hardest work you'll ever do as a parent may be the work of making the choice to encourage—the work of resisting the temptation to react in anger, of choosing words that encourage change instead of permissively accepting the status quo, of helping your children see themselves and their circumstances through the eyes of God's sanctifying love.

The power of an encouraging word to heal a family member's bitterness or apathetic heart is simply amazing. Advice columnist Ann Landers was once asked to share the most common question she received amid the millions submitted. Her answer: "What's wrong with me?"* Millions of us grow up with a secret sense of failure, and those who are closest to us, our family, have the power to turn that around. When you choose to encourage, those words have an awesome and lasting power for every person in your family. They also have the power to bring healing to your family. They bring sweetness to our dispositions and therefore to the atmosphere of our homes.

Don't forget that one of the most encouraging things

---

* Cited in Ken Durham, *Speaking from the Heart* (Fort Worth, Tex.: Worthy, 1986), 127.

you can do is to stop speaking and choose to listen. There is something deeply encouraging in the fact that someone else will listen to me, will take the time to hear about my joys and pains, my highs and lows, my victories and sorrows. James reminds us, "My dear brothers, take note of this: Everyone should be quick to listen, slow to speak and slow to become angry" (James 1:19).

I clearly remember a lesson I learned from my children. I was sitting in my home office answering e-mail, and Chaundel sat beside me and said, "I want to tell you something." I stopped working on e-mail and turned my office chair to face her. Two of our kids were in the room, and they said, "Whoa! We've never seen that before." Complete surprise — because they had never seen me stop, turn, and listen. My usual mode was to "listen while doing," making comments along the way. The reaction of my kids was embarrassing. It reminded me of a real lack in my listening skills. If you want to deeply encourage someone with your listening, you must *look at them* as you listen. Otherwise, how will they know if you're hearing them? To be truthful, if you're not looking at them, you're listening with only a part of yourself.

Jesus serves as a great example for us. With all that was on his mind as God in human flesh, he took the time to look at people as he listened to them.

> Jesus looked at them and said, "With man this is impossible, but with God all things are possible." (Matthew 19:26)
>
> Then he looked at those seated in a circle around him and said ... (Mark 3:34)
>
> Jesus looked at him and loved him. (Mark 10:21)

These are just a few examples of a pattern of compassion in Jesus' life. He listened and he looked, and then he spoke. When Jesus spoke, he spoke encouragement into the lives of all who would listen to him.

Before this day's consideration of encouraging words comes to an end, there is the promise of a life-transforming moment in looking at the way Jesus encouraged with his words. Read the words of Jesus, and you will find absolutely zero thought of "I need to just use nice politically correct words so I don't hurt anyone's feelings." Instead, Jesus said things like, "You of little faith," and "Why do you still doubt?" Jesus' encouragement was not of the brand that ignored the problem. Instead, he faced the problem head-on. Then he encouraged. To those who struggled with faith, he encouraged, "If you have just a little faith, just as much as a tiny mustard seed, you'll be able to do anything God wants." To those who struggled with their pride, he encouraged, "Stop chasing after greatness; I want to do great things in your life, if only you will depend on me with a childlike heart." To those who struggled with forgiveness, he said, "Unforgiveness ruins your relationship with God. My forgiveness of you will give you the power to forgive others." Instead of settling for negative criticism, instead of serving up feel-good platitudes, Jesus offered the gift of honest encouragement.

We get to offer to our children the same gift of honest encouragement. When our middle school child disobeys, the easy thing to say is, "*What* were you thinking?" Instead, we have the opportunity to say, "I know you made a bad choice, and I also know you have a tender heart to see that it was a bad choice. So let's talk about how you can have the faith to make a different choice next time."

Researchers have uncovered what they call the Pollyanna principle, which states that the brain processes information that is pleasing in a more precise manner than it processes unpleasant information.* In other words, we tend to tune out negative words and more easily hear positive words. This principle has strong implications for our communication with our children. As important as this is, there is an even more important principle for parents: the Jesus principle. We need his power to say the right thing. It's one thing to know that encouraging words are good; it's quite another to find that God in his love gives us the power to say these words, even when we are upset or tired.

## Response from the Heart of a Mom

*I tend to say whatever I think whenever I think of it. It's amazing, though, how the right word at the right time can change a child's heart or lift their spirits. I worked hard at being positive with my words when our children were preschoolers, but as they grew up I was tempted to be lazy with my words, thinking they could handle the negative comments. Nothing could be further from the truth.*

*A word about listening. It was my wise teenage son who said to me one day about his younger brother, "Momma, if you want Luke to talk to you about girls when he's a teenager, then you have to listen to him now about video games."*

---

\* See Margaret W. Matlin and David J. Stang, *The Pollyanna Principle: Selectivity in Language, Memory, and Thought* (Cambridge, Mass.: Schenkman, 1978).

WEEK 3, DAY 12: **What to Say When Your Child Is Struggling**

- **Verse to remember:** "You know that we dealt with each of you as a father deals with his own children, encouraging, comforting and urging you to live lives worthy of God" (1 Thessalonians 2:11–12).

- **Action to take:** Take some extra time to listen to your children today, making eye contact with them as you listen.

- **Tomorrow:** What to say when your child is angry

# What to Say When Your Child Is Angry

How do you break the cycle of yelling and arguing that seems to infect too many families today? It's natural—even healthy—for families to disagree. But it is hurtful for this disagreement to always end with loud words so that all we are left with is the emotion of anger.

As parents, we need to remember that anger is an emotion that has powerful physical characteristics. With it comes the famous "fight or flight" response, a response that pumps adrenaline into our system. Once you or your children are hit with the emotion of anger, it is impossible to say, "Just don't feel angry." The adrenaline has been released, and it has to go somewhere.

Anger is a complex emotion. There is so much more to it than the immediate adrenaline experience. The ways we choose to respond in anger quickly become our anger patterns. One of the key truths behind the principle for this week is that communication patterns become extremely hard to break. Whether your pattern is a cold stare, a slow burn, a sarcastic jab, or an explosive outburst, that response becomes your regular choice. We react to each other in ways that become quite predictable, and all too often these predictable patterns become deeply hurtful and even destructive.

How do we parents help our children when they feel anger? I love the honest encouragement our heavenly Father gives: "A gentle answer turns away wrath, but a harsh word stirs up anger" (Proverbs 15:1). Anger is a multiplying emotion. Angry responses to angry words multiply feelings of anger even more. God tells us how to change the equation by using gentle words.

Anger + anger = multiplied anger

Anger + gentle words = an opportunity for God to work

How do you break the cycle? Start with you, for you can have an effect on everyone around you. Exchange your harsh words for gentle ones. There is an awesome power in your gentle words!

The only way to speak with gentle words is out of a gentle heart. Remember the words of Jesus: "The things that come out of the mouth come from the heart" (Matthew 15:18). The only way to choose your words and to change your words is to deal first with your heart. As a parent, your choice to cultivate a gentle heart will have a lifelong impact on your children.

I don't know of any stronger or clearer statement about the power of gentleness than Jesus' words at the beginning of the Sermon on the Mount: "Blessed are the gentle, for they shall inherit the earth" (Matthew 5:5 NASB). I also don't know if there is any more misunderstood statement.

We have a perception problem with what Jesus said— a problem that centers on our understanding of the word *gentle*. Many translations use the word *meek* — which makes it even worse. Meek? Who wants to be meek? Meek means weak. Meek means geek. We don't want to be like J. Upton Dickson, the guy who founded a group called DOORMATS — Dependent Organization Of Really Meek And Timid Souls. Their motto: "The meek shall inherit the earth ... if that's OK with everybody."*

Yet Jesus said, "Blessed are the meek, the gentle." God obviously has an entirely different power scheme in mind than the one we typically endorse. Just take a look at Jesus. Jesus was gentle and humble of heart. The gentle Jesus had the power to calm a storm with just a word. Jesus Christ marched into the temple that had been turned into a marketplace and overturned the tables where the wares were being sold. Jesus openly confronted the hypocrisy of the religious leaders who were burdening God's people. Obviously God has an entirely different definition of *gentleness* than the one we have.

*Gentle* doesn't mean "quiet." It doesn't mean you swallow your anger and live with anxiety. *Gentle* means "power under control." Think of the Hoover Dam. The water behind that huge dam is under control, and when the water is sent through the dam, it creates large amounts of power and electricity. The energy to light a city is created because the power is under control. Picture a rocket launching off the pad. The power can create a huge explosion and mass destruction; but when under control, it launches the rocket into space. This is what God wants to do in your life.

As a parent, you have power in your relationship with your children. When this power is out of control, it's

---

*Cited in R. Kent Hughes, *Colossians and Philemon: The Supremacy of Christ* (Wheaton, Ill.: Crossway, 1989), 103.

destructive; when it's under control, God does amazing things. But how do you get it under control? If you've ever tried to say the right thing, only to find the wrong words coming out of your mouth, you know that this question is really when life meets reality. The answer to this question is at the core of developing the gentle response that helps our child deal with their anger.

There are three ways to live life with the power that God has given you. The first is the *out of control life*. It's about me doing whatever I feel like doing in that moment; a life marked by anger, without discipline, an explosion waiting to happen. You can live that way, and your family might not even say anything to you about it because they are afraid of the next explosion.

A second way to live is what I would call the *in control life*. You think, "I'm not supposed to be angry," so you're always in control. You're always in this little box of your own control. Maybe you're miserable inside that box, but at least you're keeping it all contained; you're keeping it all under control. That's not the kind of life God made us to live either. Those who live this life often end up religiously going through the motions until one day it all crashes in on them.

You were not made to live the *out of control life* or the *in control life* but the *under God's control life*! It is an entirely different kind of life—a life of genuine joy and adventure and hope. It is the genuinely gentle life. Blessed are the gentle, for they inherit the earth. Gentleness prevails in the end. The thing we never think would win is the thing that does win because it's where the real power is.

With a gentle heart, we're ready to put into practice the choice to give a gentle answer when we're confronted with someone's anger. In the moment of anger, the power to respond with gentleness comes from knowing that gentleness is where the real power is.

If you want to see if you're able to be gentle, just let somebody throw some confrontational words at you. Let somebody throw a zinger at you as you feel the heat rising in the back of your neck. If instead of making the choice to zing them back you make the choice to love, you know the power of living under God's control.

Suppose you're planning a quiet evening at home. Somewhere near the beginning of the evening, somebody says something that starts the temperature rising. You're suddenly on the down escalator of communication. We've all been there. Once it starts, it's difficult to stop. Proverbs 17:14 (GW) reads, "Starting a quarrel is like opening a floodgate, so stop before the argument gets out of control." How do you stop it? How do you break the cycle? Gentleness is the answer.

Let's bring back into focus the word from God with which we started today: "A gentle answer turns away wrath, but harsh words cause quarrels" (Proverbs 15:1 LB). God is saying it starts with you. If you're having an argument, whether with your spouse or your children, it will always *feel* like it is their fault. If the communication is going to change, it's going to start with you deciding to give a gentle answer. It's going to start with you defusing the situation.

This is not an issue of loud versus soft words. You can be scathingly harsh in a quiet way. It's not about how loud you are; it's about the words you choose. I have a word I often use when I disagree with Chaundel. It's not a loud word; it's just a single word that harshly communicates that I'm not agreeing. The word is "Fine!" I've practiced this word. I can fit more negativity into this one little word than many can put into entire paragraphs!

Gentle doesn't mean I just lower my voice; it means I humble my heart. It involves recognizing where I'm wrong. It means I stop assigning blame and start accepting responsibility. It is tough to say, "I was wrong," especially when the heat is rising in the back of my neck. It takes great power, God's power, to make this choice. In our family, for about fifteen years now, we've had a little thing we do to get over the hump of admitting we're wrong—because it's hard for us to do. To the tune of "Camptown Races" we sing the words, "You were right and I was wrong, doo-dah, doo-dah." When it's starting to dawn on us that the other person just may be right this time, it's a song that helps us get out of the quicksand of pride that keeps us from admitting we were wrong. Gentleness helps us to admit our own faults, which turns away wrath. Gentleness also helps us to have the compassion to see that we all struggle with our faults.

Dealing with the reality of the anger patterns in your family comes down to simple, practical things. Find ways that work for you to say, "I was wrong." Find ways to break through the barriers that are created when you push each other's buttons, so that when you're confronted you can make the choice to love. Write notes or go for a walk or sing a silly song or go out for coffee together: choose a habit or pattern or practice that works for you to give a gentle answer.

I know some of you are thinking, "It won't work for me. It won't work in my family. You don't understand. The person I'm trying to communicate with, they will not listen. I have to yell as loud as I can, and only then do I sometimes get through." Proverbs 25:15 (NCV) offers great encourage-

ment: "A gentle word can get through to the hard-headed."
If you yell, it just makes a person more stubbornly resistant.
Gentleness has the greatest chance of creating change.

There's a great prayer in the book of Psalms for those of
us who want to speak with gentler, less harsh words. "Lord,
help me control my tongue; help me be careful about what
I say" (Psalm 141:3 NCV). You know that old saying about
counting to ten when you get angry? I encourage you to
count to 141:3 the next time you get angry. Pray, *Lord, help
me control my tongue; help me be careful about what I say.
When I'm confronted, help me express gentle love.* That's the
"inherit the earth" choice.

### Response from the Heart of a Mom

*I'm embarrassed to say that all three of our children
handle the "gentle words" category much better than I
do. They must have learned from their father! My most
vivid example of this was when I was in the middle of a
verbal battle with our oldest child (he was about nine or
ten) when correcting him for some act of disobedience.
I finally exploded with the words "You are acting like
a child!" He was clearly more in control as he gently
responded, "Momma, I am a child." His gentle words
melted my angry heart.*

WEEK 3, DAY 13: **What to Say When Your Child Is Angry**

- **Verse to remember:** "Blessed are the gentle, for they shall inherit the earth" (Matthew 5:5 NASB).

- **Action to take:** When you get angry this week, count to 141:3 by repeating the words of this verse to yourself.

- **Tomorrow:** What to say when your child is deciding

# What to Say When Your Child Is Deciding

Every one of us has a Forrest Gump–sized dream for our parenting. Forrest's famous line in the movie was, "My momma always said, 'Life was like a box of chocolates. You never know what you're gonna get.'" It is our dream that after we are in heaven, our children will still be living on the pearls of wisdom we passed along to them, quoting us at appropriate times.

While this dream may be more about movies than real life, there is no doubt that parents have the opportunity to pass wisdom along to their children. As we focus on words that fit the moment this week, the moments of life when your wisdom will be most important to your children is when they are making decisions. Decisions are all about values, whether your child is deciding how to spend the dollar they got from Grandma for their third birthday or deciding what college to attend.

We pass along wisdom through our example, through the way *we* make decisions. We also pass along wisdom through our words, through the way *we help our children* make decisions. Let's consider three practical tips for the way we use our words to help our children learn wisdom: speak at the right time; speak in the right way; and choose the right words.

## 1. Speak at the Right Time.

"People enjoy giving good advice. Saying the right word at the right time is so pleasing" (Proverbs 15:23 NCV). "The right word spoken at the right time is as beautiful as gold apples in a silver bowl" (Proverbs 25:11 NCV). Speaking to your kids is like playing music: if you don't have the right sense of timing, you can play the right notes and yet always sound out of sync.

The right time to pass along wisdom to your children is when they are listening. If they've just asked you a question, this is often the perfect time to respond. We can't always interrupt what we are doing to answer our children's questions or we'd be dispensing answers all day long. Yet there are those moments when we know they're asking an important question, and so choosing to stop what we're doing to talk with them will make all the difference. I have to admit this is often harder than it should be because I'm caught up in what I want to get done at that moment and I would rather wait until a more opportune time to respond. The opportune time is usually *now*. It is true, however, that sometimes it's just not possible to talk at that moment, and so you have to find another time. With young children, it can often be at bedtime—when they would love to keep you talking so they don't have to go to sleep. With teenagers, it can be when they get home from school and are trying to avoid digging into homework or on a weekend afternoon.

## 2. Speak in the Right Way.

The secret to helping your children learn wisdom as you talk with them is to avoid making the decision; instead, *guide* the decision. Providing guidance is one of the greatest skills of relational parents. You can make the wisest decisions for your children every day of their lives—ever diligent and ever knowing—and not pass this wisdom along unless your children are encouraged in making these decisions themselves. Teaching your kids to make their own decisions takes great patience—the kind of patience God displays toward us and is willing to give to us.

When our children were small, we would occasionally have pizza at a restaurant where the kids could play little games and win tickets for whacking a mole or knocking over pins—tickets they could turn in to get a prize. How to spend those tickets was a bigger decision for them than it was for us. When we were ready to go home, they were wrestling with the decision of whether to walk out with a stuffed monkey or a big blue lollipop. In these moments, everything in us as parents wants to say, "It's really not very important in the light of eternity. Just decide!" Yet for our children, these kinds of decisions can feel as important as when we are picking out our next car. The questions we take the time to ask our children in these simple moments can give them wisdom for life—questions like "What would you really like? Are you choosing what *you* want or what your sister told you to get?" and comments like "It's time to decide now, and it's OK if you don't make the perfect choice." A few times we even saw one of our children give another the tickets they needed to get what they wanted —now *that's* life wisdom.

Your help in making these small decisions earns you the right to help in making the big decisions. Parents want to jump in when making a decision about a college or a marriage partner—certainly very important decisions. But for a thirteen-year-old, what to wear to a party is *the* most important decision; for an eight-year-old, what toy to buy with Christmas money is *the* most important decision.

Applying wisdom at a preschool level is one thing. What about when your children reach their teen years? What about those times when you do everything you can to guide them the right way, and they stubbornly want to go in a direction you know will devastate their future? Guiding toward the right decision does not mean there will not be times when you must make a decision your child won't like. Even in these moments, you can still pass along wisdom by telling your child why you are making this decision. He or she may not appreciate it at the time. They may never thank you for it, but it is the very wisdom they will one day pass along to their children.

## 3. Choose the Right Words.

Certain words give more wisdom than others. As a dad, I want to believe a twenty-minute monologue will instill wisdom in my children—that they'll take notes and file them for future reference. The truth is, the greater wisdom often comes in the questions we ask. Look at the example of Jesus. Jesus, as God in human flesh, had an eternity of wisdom to give; yet he often used questions to help people discern God's life-giving direction. "What do you want me to do for you?" he would ask. "Why are you so afraid?" "Who do you say I am?" "Why all this commotion and wailing?" "How many loaves do you have?"*—all questions that brought greater wisdom when people gave their answers.

Questions are a great way to provide guidance, but we parents want to offer more than just questions. The good news is that we have *God's wisdom* to share. To give your children a lifetime of wisdom, teach them to turn to God's Word as they make decisions. Show them where God's truth intersects with their lives.

I asked a group of parents to give me specific verses from God's Word that had helped their children make good decisions in specific circumstances. Maybe their answers will encourage and help you.

> **When irritated with a sibling.** "Do not repay evil with evil or insult with insult, but with blessing, because to this you were called so that you may inherit a blessing" (1 Peter 3:9).

> **When worried—about anything from a test to clothes that don't look right.** "Do not be anxious about anything, but in everything, by prayer and petition, with thanksgiving, present your requests to God" (Philippians 4:6).

> **When afraid—of the dark or of a new situation.** "I command you—be strong and courageous! Do not be afraid or discouraged. For the LORD your God is with you wherever you go" (Joshua 1:9 NLT). "When I am afraid, I put my trust in you" (Psalm 56:3).

> **When needing to trust that God has a path specifically designed for them.** "Trust in the LORD with all your heart and lean not on your own understanding; in all your ways acknowledge him,

---

*Mark 10:36; 4:40; 8:29; 5:39; 6:38.

and he will make your paths straight" (Proverbs 3:5–6).

**When needing to shift focus from problems to God.**
"Seek first his kingdom and his righteousness, and all these things will be given to you as well" (Matthew 6:33).

**When reconciling a relationship with a stepparent.**
"I live by faith in the Son of God, who loved me and gave himself for me" (Galatians 2:20).

**When deciding what to do or what to choose.**
"Whatever you do, work at it with all your heart, as working for the Lord, not for men, since you know that you will receive an inheritance from the Lord as a reward. It is the Lord Christ you are serving" (Colossians 3:23–24).

**When choosing friends.** "Finally, brothers, whatever is true, whatever is noble, whatever is right, whatever is pure, whatever is lovely, whatever is admirable—if anything is excellent or praiseworthy—think about such things" (Philippians 4:8).

**When deciding to trust Jesus for salvation.** "God so loved the world that he gave his one and only Son, that whoever believes in him shall not perish but have eternal life" (John 3:16).

**When something good has happened.** "Give thanks to the LORD, for he is good; his love endures forever" (Psalm 107:1).

**When faced with temptation.** "Flee from all this, and pursue righteousness, godliness, faith, love, endurance and gentleness" (1 Timothy 6:11).

**When facing conflict.** "Everyone should be quick to listen, slow to speak and slow to become angry" (James 1:19).

**When being bullied.** "I will say of the LORD, 'He is my refuge and my fortress, my God, in whom I trust'" (Psalm 91:2).

**When setting priorities and making goals.** "So be careful how you live, not as fools but as those who are wise ... Don't act thoughtlessly, but try to understand what the Lord wants you to do" (Ephesians 5:15, 17 NLT).

**When facing doubt.** "If anyone chooses to do God's will, he will find out whether my teaching comes from God or whether I speak on my own" (John 7:17).

**When being picked on for being a Christian.** "Who is going to harm you if you are eager to do good? But even if you should suffer for what is right, you are blessed. 'Do not fear what they fear; do not be frightened.' But in your hearts set apart Christ as Lord. Always be prepared to give an answer to everyone who asks you to give the reason for the hope that you have. But do this with gentleness and respect" (1 Peter 3:13 – 15).

**When rushing into a decision.** "Plans fail for lack of counsel, but with many advisers they succeed" (Proverbs 15:22).

**When feeling inadequate.** "We are God's workmanship, created in Christ Jesus to do good works, which God prepared in advance for us to do" (Ephesians 2:10).

**When feeling overwhelmed.** "Come to me, all you who are weary and burdened, and I will give you rest" (Matthew 11:28).

**And the favorite verse of parents for their children.** "I can do everything through him who gives me strength" (Philippians 4:13).

Of course, you have to be careful as you teach Bible verses to your children. One parent whose preschooler had just memorized Ephesians 4:32 told me that as she was disciplining him, he said, "Be kind to one another." Mom responded with another verse: "Children, obey your parents." Her son had the last word when he quoted, "Do what is right in the eyes of the Lord."

Wisdom is passed on to our children as we speak at the right time and in the right way, and as we choose the right words. More than anything, wisdom is passed on as we share how the wisdom in God's Word has impacted our lives and how it can apply in the very circumstances that your child faces today.

### Response from the Heart of a Mom

*Timing has never been my strong suit—especially when it comes to wise words. If I have a thought, I want to share it now! It's amazing the difference in impact and response when a rightly timed word is spoken. When they are listening instead of when I want to say it— what a novel thought! I want my kids to listen to my wise words on my timetable, but a truly wise word for my child about a decision they are making can wait for the right time. From my perspective, the decision is usually clear and I just want to lay it all out, but if I am willing to wait for the right timing, my children are better prepared to come to a strong decision on their own.*

WEEK 3, DAY 14: **What to Say When Your Child Is Deciding**

- **Verse to remember:** "The right word spoken at the right time is as beautiful as gold apples in a silver bowl" (Proverbs 25:11 NCV).

- **Action to take:** Share with your child one of the Bible verses from today's reading that fits a circumstance they are facing.

- **Tomorrow:** What to say when your child is anxious

# What to Say When Your Child Is Anxious

As we look back on our childhood, many of us remember a minefield of anxieties. In grade school it was the bully on the playground or the math test on fractions that had our stomach churning; in high school it was wondering if we made the team or what we would do after we graduated. Children often feel powerless as they face an unknown future—and this sets them up for that feeling we call worry.

What can we do to help our children overcome their worries? God gives wisdom for us in the book of Proverbs —wisdom that offers simple and clear direction for what to say when someone is anxious. "An anxious heart weighs a man down, but a kind word cheers him up" (Proverbs 12:25). When your child is worried, speak kindly.

Kind words bring a smile to a person's heart. They have the power to point us to the goodness of God. This verse reveals the truth that kind words can take the problem of worry and translate it into joy. Anyone in your family have a problem with worry? You can make a real difference by choosing to speak kindly.

What exactly is "a kind word"? Kindness is caring about the details. It is a concern for another person that reaches its way even to the smallest details of that person's life. Why is kindness so powerful? It is the way we communicate that we really care. And when we know someone cares, we can find a security that produces joy and defeats worry —because we know we are not facing our struggles alone.

I have to admit that when faced with someone else's worry, my first response is often anything but kindness. My worries seem so very important; your worries seem inconsequential and even silly. It is easy to minimize the anxieties our children are feeling. "Stop worrying about that test; believe me, you'll have a lot bigger things to worry about when you're my age." If we don't say it, we often think it. When we set aside these thoughts and intentionally choose kindness, it can make all the difference in reducing our children's anxiety.

We all know it is good to be kind. Most of us want to choose to be kind. Why, then, do we so often find unkind words spilling from our mouths? How do we begin to choose kindness more often in our everyday conversations and actions?

It's a matter of focus. Most of the time, I'm focused on myself—my needs, my schedule, my priorities, my world. It is simply impossible to offer simple kindness to anyone as long as I am focused on myself. Kindness by its very definition requires that I think about their needs and not my own.

So how do you get the focus off yourself? The answer to that question is the secret to kindness. Two truths will make the difference and change your focus: (1) your identity is in Christ, and (2) God's focus is on you. These two truths may seem unrelated to words of kindness, yet it is in knowing these truths about yourself that you are given the power to be kind to others.

## 1. Your identity is in Christ.

To get the focus off yourself, you must have some sense of security in who you really are. Otherwise, you'll constantly be focusing on yourself in an attempt to feel better about yourself. You are set free to care for others — your children or anyone else — when you realize that your identity, the core of who you are, is found in your relationship with Jesus.

Some parents take the unhealthy path of minimizing themselves and becoming codependent. A codependent parent has made their child so important that their only identity is now in their parenting. No parent wants to admit they are codependent, yet I have found that every one of us who tries to succeed at parenting can take a trip down that road all too easily. If you've ever been to a Little League game where you've heard a parent yelling at the umpire and then thought, "I'd never even *think* of doing that" — you may not have faced some realities about yourself. If you've told yourself, "There's no way I would base any feelings of self-worth on the college my child gets into," you may need an honest conversation with your soul. If your child is at Harvard, you tend to include that fact in your conversations much more often than if they're at the local community college! These natural tendencies can all too easily grow into codependent thinking. It's one of the greatest dangers that "good parents" face.

Thankfully, God gives us the answer: *find your greater identity in Christ*. Once you become a believer, God begins to see you for who you are "in Christ." You are in Christ if Christ is in you. An exchange of life occurs. You give Jesus your life, and he gives you his. You become a new person—and that is where your identity is now found. You don't find your identity in your parenting or in your job; it is found in Christ. Below is a list of who you now are because of Jesus. Who is this "new person"?

- I am a light in the world (Matthew 5:14).

- I am a child of God (John 1:12).

- I am a friend of Jesus (John 15:15).

- I am chosen and appointed by Jesus to bear his fruit (John 15:16).

- I am a slave to righteousness (Romans 6:18).

- I am a co-heir with Christ (Romans 8:17).

- I am a temple, a dwelling place, of God (1 Corinthians 3:16; 6:19).

- I am a member of Christ's body (1 Corinthians 12:27; Ephesians 5:30).

- I am a new creation (2 Corinthians 5:17).

- I am reconciled to God and a minister of reconciliation (2 Corinthians 5:18–19).

- I am a saint (1 Corinthians 1:2; Ephesians 1:1).

- I am God's workmanship (Ephesians 2:10).

- I am a citizen of heaven (Ephesians 2:6; Philippians 3:20).

- I am righteous and holy (Ephesians 4:24).

- I am hidden with Christ in God (Colossians 3:3).

- I am chosen and dearly loved (Colossians 3:12).

- I am a child of light and not of darkness (1 Thessalonians 5:5).

- I am an enemy of the Devil (1 Peter 5:8).

- I am victorious (1 John 5:4).

- I am born again (1 Peter 1:23).

- I am alive with Christ (Ephesians 2:5).

- I am more than a conqueror (Romans 8:37).

- I am the righteousness of God (2 Corinthians 5:21).

- I am born of God, and the Evil One cannot touch me (1 John 5:18).

- I am to be like Christ when he returns (1 John 3:2).*

To get the focus off yourself, recognize that your identity is in Christ. And realize, too, that there is a second choice that empowers kindness in your life.

## 2. God's focus is on you.

Read Psalm 139, and you quickly realize that God's focus is on you.

> O LORD, you have searched me
>     and you know me.
> You know when I sit and when I rise;
>     you perceive my thoughts from afar.
> You discern my going out and my lying down;
>     you are familiar with all my ways.
> Before a word is on my tongue
>     you know it completely, O LORD.

---

*Adapted from Tom Holladay and Kay Warren, *Foundations: 11 Core Truths to Build Your Life On*, vol. 2 of the Teacher's Guide (Grand Rapids: Zondervan, 2003), 60–61.

You hem me in—behind and before;
   you have laid your hand upon me.

                                                PSALM 139:1-5

Read the words of Jesus, and you can't miss the wonder of God's care for you:

"Look at the birds of the air; they do not sow or reap or store away in barns, and yet your heavenly Father feeds them. Are you not much more valuable than they? Who of you by worrying can add a single hour to his life?

"And why do you worry about clothes? See how the lilies of the field grow. They do not labor or spin. Yet I tell you that not even Solomon in all his splendor was dressed like one of these. If that is how God clothes the grass of the field, which is here today and tomorrow is thrown into the fire, will he not much more clothe you, O you of little faith? So do not worry, saying, 'What shall we eat?' or 'What shall we drink?' or 'What shall we wear?'"

                                                MATTHEW 6:26-31

When I see that God's heart is turned toward me, I am able to turn my heart toward others. When I see God's kindness toward me, I am able to speak and act with kindness toward others.

The healthy way to get the focus off yourself is to realize that God's focus is on you—and on your children and on everyone else in this world. The focus gets off myself when I realize God's focus is on all of us, that we live together under his loving care. Instead of being independent or codependent, I realize we are all mutually dependent on him.

With this sense of us standing together and depending on God, there will come a refreshing freedom to be kind to others. I then realize how kind God has been to me—in spite of all those times I did not deserve it or acted as if I didn't need it. God's kindness toward me motivates my kindness toward others, my kindness toward my family. And then I find genuine power to speak kind words to my children when they are facing worries. This kindness will then help my children let go of their worries as they realize that they are not alone, that someone else cares, and that they can talk to God and trust him with any and all of the details of their lives.

### Response from the Heart of a Mom

*It's so tempting to dismiss children's anxieties. They seem so—childish! When you compare them to our adult worries, they seem so insignificant, as if we have a "right" to worry—which we don't. In those times when my children worry, I am often impatient. There are times when I want to brush aside their worries by saying, "Come on, get over it! Just trust God." If I instead take time to understand their worries and speak kindly, God is often able to use me to alleviate their worries. For me, there is something about spending time alone with God as I speak honestly with him about my worries and hear his kind words to me that empowers me to speak kind words to my children.*

WEEK 3, DAY 15: **What to Say When Your Child Is Anxious**

- **Verse to remember:** "An anxious heart weighs a man down, but a kind word cheers him up" (Proverbs 12:25).

- **Action to take:** Choose kindness today by expressing interest in the details of something that interests your child.

- **Next week:** Parenting Principle #4: Show and teach mercy.

# Show and Teach Mercy

## The Power of Your Discipline and Compassion

And now a word to you parents. Don't keep on scolding and nagging your children, making them angry and resentful. Rather, bring them up with the loving discipline the Lord himself approves, with suggestions and godly advice.

Ephesians 6:4 LB

Parents, don't come down too hard on your children or you'll crush their spirits.

Colossians 3:21 MSG

# We All Need Mercy

In Matthew 7, Jesus deals with three issues that are vital to every family—hypocrisy, integrity, and mercy. These issues are learned and experienced in the closeness of family like nowhere else. Jesus taught us that *hypocrisy* is pointing out the speck in someone else's eye while ignoring the plank in our own eye; *integrity* is taking the plank out of our own eye; and *mercy* is removing the speck from another's eye.

"Do not judge, or you too will be judged. For in the same way you judge others, you will be judged, and with the measure you use, it will be measured to you.

"Why do you look at the speck of sawdust in your brother's eye and pay no attention to the plank in your own eye? How can you say to your brother, 'Let me take the speck out of your eye,' when all the time there is a plank in your own eye? You hypocrite, first take the plank out of your own eye, and then you will see clearly to remove the speck from your brother's eye."

MATTHEW 7:1–5

This is deeply important for parents. Jesus tells me that if I'm going to show my children mercy, I must abandon hypocrisy and pursue integrity. And then I must move outside of myself to offer the other person genuine mercy. We focus on mercy this week. Today we take a general look at the character of mercy in our lives, and then for next four days we'll drill down into how mercy is taught and shown in our homes.

Of all the qualities we can teach our children, I believe the greatest privilege as a parent may be our opportunity to teach them to have a heart of mercy. God has shown his awesome mercy to us, and we get to show our children how to express mercy toward others. The Old Testament prophet Micah wrote, "And what does the LORD require of you? To act justly and to love mercy and to walk humbly with your God" (Micah 6:8). As a parent, I ask myself, "How do I get my children to truly love mercy?" I realize it has to start with me, with how I deal with hypocrisy, choose integrity, and love mercy.

It starts with realizing our mutual need before God—a need displayed by the very first family on earth in a clear and shocking way. Imagine the day Adam came to Eve and said, "I have some terrible news about our sons." Eve and Adam's first son had been an absolute miracle to them. God had created the two of them from dust and rib, so they had never seen a baby. When Abel was born, Eve said with wide-eyed amazement, "With the help of the LORD I have brought forth a man" (Genesis 4:1). And then, perhaps with some sisters in between, a second son had come, and they had named him Cain. Growing up, there were surely signs of sibling rivalry and jealousy between these two boys, but how would Adam and Eve know if this was normal or extreme? These were the first two brothers, so no standards had yet been set.

Now the news had come to these parents. Cain, in his jealousy over God's honoring of Abel's sacrifice and not his, had killed his own brother. The parents must have felt it was all over—finished for Cain, finished for them as parents, and *certainly* finished for Abel.

They were wrong.

God continued to work lovingly in Cain's life as he confronted him over his sin, and God was present with him as he fled east of Eden. God still had work for Adam and Eve to do—even as parents—as he gave them another son in Seth. And the continued influence of Abel is seen in his being in God's Hall of Fame for people of faith in Hebrews 11. The very act of faith that caused his brother to kill him became the example of faith that is honored there: "By faith Abel offered God a better sacrifice than Cain did." (From Genesis 2–4.)

• • •

From the very beginning, we have seen that there is no such thing as a perfect person—we all need mercy. There is no such thing as a perfect family—mercy is needed in every home. In fact, it is in our families—where we cannot easily hide the realities of our sin—that we have the greatest opportunity to learn to express mercy.

Jesus used a simple speck in the eye to teach us about the everyday choices that lead to mercy. As parents, we face three questions that grow out of the teaching of Jesus every single day:

## 1. Am I teaching my children hypocrisy?

It's the easiest thing in the world to teach your children to be hypocrites. Hypocrisy is pointing out the wrong in someone else's life but being unwilling to admit to it in your own life. Hypocrisy is saying to your kids, "Do as I say and not as I do."

The word *hypocrisy* is derived from the Greek word for an actor on the stage who spoke from behind a mask held in front of his or her face. Hypocrisy is all about hiding behind a mask. It's pretending to be something you are not, and nowhere is this so easily seen as in the home.

Letting go of hypocrisy means you drop the pretense. "Don't just pretend that you love others. Really love them," wrote Paul (Romans 12:9 NLT). It's so easy to pretend. I'm shocked at how often I pretend to listen to the people I love most. My mind wanders off to something that seems so important, and I don't hear what is being said. Seeing my glassy-eyed stare, they ask, "Did you hear what I was saying?" This is the moment of truth. Do I continue to pretend, or will I come clean? Far too often I've said, "Sure, I heard you," and then tried to put together the pieces of the conversation in order to act as though I had been listening all along. Why don't I just stop pretending? It would be much more refreshing and real to say, "I'm so sorry; I wasn't listening. Please say that again."

## 2. Am I teaching my children integrity?

Integrity is not being without any faults; it's being honest about the faults you have. It is rejecting the temptation to blame others and choosing to look honestly at your own life. When you make this choice, your children cannot help but see it. Your children see your faults. The older they get, the more aware of them they become. They also see your honesty about these faults, your willingness to humbly seek to change.

Integrity shows your children what you value most. I faced this values question recently at Home Depot. I went there to buy sod to replace a section of our lawn that had died. I found a clerk, and he had me pay him for the thirty squares of sod I needed. He told me the sod was stacked in front of the store, where I could back up my van to load them. He asked if I needed any help. I told him I could load them myself. As I was putting the pieces into the van one by one, I began to wonder if I had bought enough. And then the thought hit me: *No one is watching me load this sod. Who would know if I put in one or two extra pieces—just in case? They'd probably dry up and die before the end of the day anyway!* Then another thought hit me. *This is a values question. What is more important: God or sod? Am I really going to sacrifice my integrity for a square of dirt and grass?* It made me laugh and reminded me to make the right choice. Integrity is who you are when you think no one is looking. Your children get to see this integrity because they are looking more often than you know. One of the greatest influences you will have is found in your choices of integrity that no one but your family really knows.

## 3. Am I teaching my children mercy?

Jesus told us not to judge. How do we do that? We do it by showing mercy instead. Tolerance is not enough; our world needs mercy. We live in a society that believes the opposite of judgment is tolerance. And tolerance is falsely defined as accepting without opinion or comment whatever choices another makes. Jesus teaches us the alternative to judgment is not tolerance; it is mercy. The alternative to being judgmental is not ignoring other people's faults; it is showing that Jesus has forgiven all our faults.

Being biblically nonjudgmental does not mean we pretend we don't see another person's sin. To do so would be to live in denial. Of course we see each other's sins — many of them are very obvious. The question is this: What will we do about it? Being nonjudgmental means we recognize that we all face the same temptations. It means we don't see anyone as outside the circle of God's grace, as beyond the bounds of our forgiveness, as outside the limits of our love.

The choice to reject hypocrisy and model integrity and mercy is most uniquely and powerfully seen in the home. Where else do people get to see the real you? You may be able to put up a false front for the neighbors or even for those at work, but your family knows. When you make the choice to admit a fault at the end of an argument and seek to change, you have taught a lifelong lesson about rejecting hypocrisy and choosing integrity. When you treat with kindness a waiter who has been rude to you, messed up your order, and then spilled a cup of iced tea in your lap, you've moved past talking about mercy to teaching mercy.

As we focus on mercy these next few days, we'll be looking at four powerful ways we can influence our children to have a heart of mercy: through the way we choose to not frustrate our kids, the way we discipline, the way we show compassion, and the way we forgive. We'll be talking this week about some of the hardest work of parenting and also about some of the places where you will find the greatest and most lasting rewards.*

---

*Portions of this daily reading were adapted from Tom Holladay, *The Relationship Principles of Jesus* (Grand Rapids: Zondervan, 2008), 195–221.

### *Response from the Heart of a Mom*

*These three things—hypocrisy, integrity, and mercy —caused me to think with gratitude about my own parents and how they sought to be authentic, merciful people. The iced tea in the lap illustration came from an experience when I was a girl and a server had messed up our order several times and then proceeded to spill a large glass of iced tea in my dad's lap. "Ooooh—that's cold!" he said with a smile, and then he left a large tip. That's mercy, and I'll never forget the practical example of how my dad showed it that day.*

WEEK 4, DAY 16: **We All Need Mercy**

- **Verse to remember:** "You hypocrite, first take the plank out of your own eye, and then you will see clearly to remove the speck from your brother's eye" (Matthew 7:5).

- **Action to take:** Ask the Lord to show you his mercy in new and deeper ways as we begin this week of looking at how we can teach our children mercy.

- **Tomorrow:** Stop driving your kids crazy.

# Stop Driving Your Kids Crazy

One of the most important opportunities we have as parents is the opportunity to teach our children genuine mercy. This teaching begins with us. We talked yesterday about the importance of what we model in our own actions. Equal to that in importance is the way we treat our children. Our treatment of our kids is the first place they learn about mercy and forgiveness, and so it is one of the most powerful and enduring ways they learn about mercy and forgiveness.

God knows this, and he knows how overwhelming this can be for us as parents. We think, "*Me*—teach my children about mercy, with all the struggles *I* have to forgive and accept forgiveness?" I love the practical and clear direction God gives us at this point. He knows what we cannot do: *we cannot be perfect*. He knows also what we *can* do, and he guides us into four actions we're going to look at over the next few days: first, don't exasperate your children; second, discipline your children; third, show compassion to your children; and fourth, choose forgiveness in your home.

These are the four actions we take toward our children day by day that will teach them mercy.

• • •

The teaching of mercy begins with the decision *not to exasperate your children*. You see this choice clearly in the simple words of Ephesians 6:4: "Fathers, do not exasperate your children; instead, bring them up in the training and instruction of the Lord." Don't drive your kids up the wall! These words were written to dads, possibly because they were the disciplinarians of the day or maybe because too often we dads aren't relationally sensitive in thinking through the impact of our words, but they obviously fit both moms and dads.

I cannot help but make a comment here about the truth of the Bible. These words from Paul are totally against the current of Bible times. In the first century, a Roman father had absolute control over his children. He could cast them out of the house, sell them as slaves, or even kill them with no legal penalty. A newborn would be placed at his father's feet to determine his future. If the father picked up the baby, he or she became a member of the family; if he walked away, the baby was sold. Into that kind of culture, God inspires these words about a father who cares enough about the fact that his child is a person created in God's image that he will strive not to exasperate his children.

Hear again what our heavenly Father has to say to us as parents. *The Living Bible* paraphrases it this way: "And now a word to you parents. Don't keep on scolding and nagging your children, making them angry and resentful. Rather, bring them up with the loving discipline the Lord himself approves, with suggestions and godly advice" (Ephesians

6:4). Colossians 3:21 echoes the same command: "Parents, don't come down too hard on your children or you'll crush their spirits" (Colossians 3:21 MSG).

So here's the big question: What exasperates children? Well, it's many of the same things that exasperate you about your boss at work! It's easy to become frustrated with someone who has authority over you. Here's a quick list, gathered from talking to parents who were once children, of what can frustrate our kids.

**Unclear boundaries.** Often we are just not specific enough in our directions to our children. "Don't watch too much TV," we say. How much is too much? "Five hours sounds good to me," our children decide. "Be sure to be in early," we tell our teenager. "Three in the morning *is* early," they say. "Don't wear short dresses," we say. "You call this *short*?" your daughter answers. Clear boundaries mean we say how much is too much, how late is too late, and how short is too short. Clear boundaries also mean that we are specific about what will happen if the child crosses those boundaries. Instead of saying, "You're really going to get it!" we make the consequences clear.

Instead of just reading through this list, I invite you to think about small changes you can make that will impact your kids in a big way. What can you do to make a boundary clearer—particularly one you may be struggling with at present?

**Inconsistent discipline.** Think in terms of your work. One day you get a high five for being great with people on the phone; the next day you are called on the carpet for spending too much time with customers on the phone. It's enough to drive you crazy. Our kids feel the same way when we give completely different discipline in the same situations. Our parents did the same thing to us—it's amazing that any of us turn out with a measure of emotional health!

There are many reasons we become inconsistent in our discipline. We get tired; we're distracted; we want our kids to like us. I'd much rather take my kids out for ice cream than make them stay home for a weekend to catch up on schoolwork!

Instead of striving for perfection on this one, what if we just faced up to our inconsistency as human beings? And then what if we planned to begin to discipline based on that confession? What happens when I honestly face up to the fact that I am an inconsistent, undisciplined, sinful human being who has been given responsibility by God to discipline another inconsistent, undisciplined, sinful human being? It first makes me smile at God's sense of humor. It also causes me to pause a moment before exacting discipline, because I realize I can too easily react emotionally. It creates a greater willingness to listen to other parents and even to my children. Discipline becomes more a daily relationship than just a proclamation. It may mean I more often will have a second thought and go back and give discipline where I may have let something slide by or be willing to back away from too harsh a discipline that I gave in the emotion of the moment.

Ask yourself: What will it take for me to be more consistent?

***Unbalanced criticism.*** Everything I've ever read about motivating people says you have to balance every one word of criticism with at least ten words of praise. This advice applies to parenting as much as to any other relationship. I've talked to some parents who feel that if we praise our kids too much, they'll listen only to the praise and will miss the tough words of discipline. The opposite is actually true. Without balancing words of praise, our words of correction get lost in our kids' negative feelings about themselves.

Ask yourself: What can I praise my child for this week?

***Unreasonable demands.*** We make an unreasonable demand anytime we ask a child to do something beyond their abilities. It obviously doesn't work to discipline a child to get an A in math when a B would be a miraculous achievement for them. But there is more to making unreasonable demands than this; they can also be demands we make without giving a reason. When our kids ask for a reason that they should keep some rule, we often pull out our favorite phrase as parents. I've used it myself. "Because I said so," we state with solemn strength. We want them to obey simply because it is the right thing to do.

But think for a moment about how God our Father treats us. If anyone has a right to demand obedience simply "because I said so," God does! Love one another—because I said so! Pray—because I said so! Read your Bible—because I said so! God could say this, but he usually doesn't exercise the right. Instead, he regularly tells us *why* he says so. He commands us to pray and expects our obedience; and he also tells us why prayer is so valuable to our connection with him and the doing of his will. He tells us to give sacrificially, not just "because I said so," but because the act of giving will increase our joy and is an investment in eternity.

Let's admit it: sometimes we say "because I said so" because we're tired and don't want to take the time to think through how to explain why we're asking something of our child. I'm not talking about giving a reason so they can choose not to obey if they don't like our explanation, but about giving the biblical reasons behind what we're asking them to do. They may roll their eyes at those reasons in the moment, but we're trusting that these principles will eventually sink into their souls.

***Unspoken expectations.*** Of all the potential points of frustration in the way we discipline our children, this may be the greatest. We have some expectation of what we are disciplining our child toward, but we've never spoken it — not to them and possibly not even to ourselves. We expect our two-year-old to speak in a quiet voice in the evenings, but we've never expressed it. When we speak an expectation, it gives our child a chance to see the boundary more clearly. It may have another result — we may come to see that it is an unreasonable demand. We may have an unspoken expectation that our child will attend the college we attended, yet we know the grades they're getting will not get them accepted. So we discipline them toward better grades, without ever verbalizing why. This creates great tension and frustration.

Ask yourself: What expectation do I need to speak clearly or to free my child from?

***Undeserved or unresolved anger.*** How we deal with anger is a huge issue in our families. Most of us are good at hiding our anger, but we cannot hide it from everyone, and those who see our anger are most often those in our homes. Our anger often comes out sideways. We're mad at our boss, but we yell at our kids. In an earlier chapter, we looked at the importance of honest confession after we've expressed undeserved anger.

It is also important not to allow even justifiable anger

to go unresolved. You may have expressed to your child that the lie they told makes you legitimately angry because you've been hurt by their lack of trust and you know how deeply the lie can hurt them. Even then, the anger must be resolved. If you go for days without speaking, bitterness is allowed to grow. God is clear about this because he knows our hearts so well: "Do not let the sun go down while you are still angry" (Ephesians 4:26). Admit that you're angry, and deal with it immediately. Admitting isn't easy. We tend to use all kinds of other words to describe our emotion: we're frustrated, annoyed, troubled, antagonized, exasperated, vexed, indignant, provoked, hurt, irked, irritated, cross. The truth is, we have some anger that must be dealt with.

Sleeping on anger is like sleeping on a bed of nails; you wake up feeling great pain. Let anger hang around, and it grows into bitterness. Angry words are a discordant tone in the home—a tone that needs to be resolved through another conversation before the end of the day. As you assure your children that you love them and that the anger you felt was because of your desire to protect them, they are learning lessons about mercy that cannot be learned anywhere else.

Ask yourself: Is there an angry encounter that I haven't yet resolved?

It takes great humility to admit our tendency to exasperate our children, and even greater humility to act in new ways. When you make these choices, you are teaching your children the character of mercy, passing on to them the mercy that Jesus has shown you, and helping to form a heart in them that can pass mercy on to others.

### Response from the Heart of a Mom

*The thing I struggle with most as a parent in this chapter is unspoken expectations. Just as I want my husband to figure out the perfect Christmas gift for me without my having to spell it out, I want my kids to figure out exactly what I expect from them. The truth is, I don't want to verbalize these expectations because I may have to admit that they are selfish or unrealistic. It's much easier to hang on to unrealistic or selfish expectations if they are unspoken!*

## WEEK 4, DAY 17: Stop Driving Your Kids Crazy

- **Verse to remember:** "Parents, don't come down too hard on your children or you'll crush their spirits" (Colossians 3:21 MSG).

- **Action to take:** Look again at the six ways we can exasperate our children and ask yourself what changes you can make in just one of these areas.

- **Tomorrow:** Loving discipline

# Loving Discipline

We're focusing this week on what we can do to teach our children the character of mercy. Jesus taught us, "Blessed are the merciful" (Matthew 5:7). To teach mercy to children takes much more than just saying, "Be merciful." Yesterday we looked at the power of our choice not to exasperate our children. There is a second choice we make—the choice to discipline our children. As we talk about discipline today, not only will we address questions about *how we discipline*, but we will also raise the even more important question of *why we discipline*. Once we know why we discipline, the how becomes much clearer.

Discipline is one of the greatest challenges we face as parents. I know that discussions about how to discipline in specific situations can lead to some of our greatest disagreements as parents. Those who say that discipline is easy probably have a complacent child (not a strong-willed one), and he is their only child! Aside from the Bible, I believe the greatest authority on parenting isn't Dr. Spock or Dr. Laura or Dr. Phil; it's Dr. Bill Cosby. He once said, "Having a child is surely the most beautifully irrational act that two people in love can commit."* Regarding discipline when you discover that something has been broken in your home, Cosby says we don't really experience parenthood if we only have one kid, because with one kid we always know who did it.

Paul in his letter to the Ephesians gives practical direction for the discipline of our children: "Bring them up with the loving discipline the Lord himself approves, with suggestions and godly advice" (Ephesians 6:4 LB). The way you discipline your children will be one of their greatest life lessons on mercy. Without discipline, children learn to be selfish. With the right kind of discipline, children learn integrity for themselves and compassionate mercy toward others. What is the right kind of discipline? Paul describes it with the word *loving*.

What makes discipline loving? Loving discipline is discipline that is done for the child's sake, not the parent's. The focus is on their growth, not on our needs as parents. The way God treats us is our example.

Hebrews 12 gives us guidance:

> Our fathers disciplined us for a little while as they thought best; but God disciplines us for our good, that we may share in his holiness. No discipline seems pleasant at the time, but painful. Later on, however, it produces a harvest of righteousness and peace for those who have been trained by it.
>
> HEBREWS 12:10–11

There are four principles here concerning the way God disciplines us that hold out to us great wisdom in disciplining our children.

---

*Bill Cosby, *Fatherhood* (New York: Berkley, 1987), 18.

## 1. Everyone needs to be disciplined.

We simply cannot begin to become everything God intends for us to be without some measure of discipline in our lives. God uses many ways to discipline us as his children, including allowing the natural consequences of our actions to teach us, putting the challenge of his truth before us, and placing the right person in our lives to motivate us. I would like to think that, left to myself, I would be wonderfully self-disciplined and would always do the right thing. The hard truth is that I'm much too easy on myself and tend to drift toward selfishness and laziness. If you put a doughnut and an apple in front of me, I'll probably go for the doughnut if I'm all alone; but if someone is looking, I might at least consider the apple!

## 2. Discipline is painful.

I love God's honesty about this: "No discipline seems pleasant at the time, but painful." It's the very pain of the circumstance we don't want to face or the conversation we know we'll have to face that causes us to change. We don't change when we see the light; we change when we feel the heat.

It's going to hurt when we take away media privileges or cut an allowance or give a time-out to discipline our child for a poor choice they have made. Trying to discipline without some discomfort for the child is like trying to lose weight without changing our diet or exercise routine.

The number one question I hear concerning this issue is whether there is ever a place for physical discipline of children. What about spanking? The Bible says it is an acceptable form of discipline, but I don't believe it is a required form of discipline. This is where you have to know the circumstance—as well as know your child and yourself. In certain circumstances, a slap on the hand may be the only thing that keeps a small child from being burned by a hot stove. Some children just will not listen to the discipline of reason or loss of privilege, but the possibility of a spanking will change their direction. Some parents find themselves spanking as an expression of their anger, which only creates more anger and no true discipline. Chaundel and I chose to use spanking to discipline our children very rarely when they were younger—and then only for willful and clear acts of disobedience. As they grew older, other forms of discipline became much better choices for us. Every parent must prayerfully choose how to discipline based on an understanding of themselves and their children.

There is a more important question about discipline today than whether or not to spank. The question is: Will I allow my children to face the natural consequences of their actions? It is tempting to want to rescue our child from an "unfair discipline" handed down by a teacher or a coach or even a boss. We hate to see our kids hurt and feel that any discipline they receive should come from us as parents and no one else. Actually, the most important discipline they receive often comes from outside of the home. Discipline is experienced in both the *corrections* we give and the *consequences* we allow. One of the most difficult choices we make is to allow these natural consequences to unfold instead of always bailing out our children.

## 3. Discipline is for my kids' benefit, not my benefit.

"God disciplines us for our good." This is the way I want

to discipline my children—*for their good*. Have you ever disciplined your kids more for your benefit than for theirs? I sure have. Years ago, we were putting out our manger scenes at Christmas—Chaundel has quite a collection from all over the world. Our daughter, Alyssa, early elementary age at the time, asked if she could put a fragile, breakable little baby Jesus into the manger. I told her it was so small that it might too easily drop. "Please, Daddy," she said, "I'll be careful." "OK," I told her, "but just don't drop it." My stern warning almost guaranteed the result, and the baby Jesus slipped from her fingers and broke in two on the marble floor. I groaned my deep disappointment and said to Alyssa something like, "Go to your room and think about what you did." I disciplined her, but it was for *my* benefit, not hers. The truth is, I was most upset about the task of trying to superglue that baby Jesus back together. Later I apologized to her, and we glued Jesus back together again. We even noticed that there was now a little superglue tear coming out of his porcelain eye.

Love is focusing on someone else's need and not merely your own. Loving discipline is done *for the child's sake*, not for the parent's sake.

Let's dig into this a bit. If you and your spouse agree you want your home to be a quiet place, this is your completely valid right. And if your children are willfully disobeying your instructions to be quiet—you can tell by the defiant gleam in the eye—then they need to be disciplined to respect your wishes. But there are times when it's not willful disobedience; it's just that one of your children is naturally louder than the others. God gave your other children piccolo and clarinet voices—but one child has a trombone voice! Constantly disciplining this child to be like your other children can easily become more for your sake than for theirs. One of the greatest heart challenges for any parent is distinguishing between asking for something I need and disciplining for their good. There is absolutely nothing wrong with asking for what you need; you just need to remember that it's different from disciplining for their good.

## 4. My short-term discipline should prepare my children for God's lifetime discipline.

Hebrews 12 draws the clear distinction between us and God. We discipline for a short time as we think best; God disciplines for all of our lives in order to bring qualities such as righteousness and peace into our lives. As a parent, I'm just the first part of the lifetime process of God's discipline in my children's lives. To me, there is something freeing about this. It's not as if it is all on my shoulders and I must discipline my children in a way that prepares them for *everything* they'll face in life. I don't know all they will face, but God does; and he asks us to discipline as we think best, doing it all out of the motivation of love. You may want to pray a prayer like this one:

> *Father, I don't know all that my children will face and will need in life; but you do. Lead me to discipline them in a way that prepares their hearts for what you give them to do in the world and in a way that protects their hearts from what the evil world could do to them. In Jesus' name, amen.*

### Response from the Heart of a Mom

*Oh my! This chapter brings back for me a lot of memories—mostly ones in which I'm feeling angry or frustrated with one of our children and wanting to lash out and discipline them to meet my needs. Fortunately, in our home Tom had a much longer fuse and could help me take a deep breath and a step back before disciplining in haste. It definitely comforts me to realize I'm not the only source of discipline in my children's lives. And I'm also encouraged to open myself up to God's discipline in my own life so that he can produce a harvest of righteousness and peace in and through me.*

WEEK 4, DAY 18: **Loving Discipline**

- **Verse to remember:** "Bring them up with the loving discipline the Lord himself approves, with suggestions and godly advice" (Ephesians 6:4 LB).

- **Action to take:** Stop right now to ask God to give you wisdom for the disciplining of your children.

- **Tomorrow:** The gift of compassion

# The Gift of Compassion

We're looking this week at how we express the all-important character of mercy in our homes. As God encourages us to show and teach mercy, he urges us first to stop exasperating our children and then to lovingly discipline our children. Today we'll look at a third choice that guides us toward mercy—the decision to show compassion.

David writes, "As a father has compassion on his children, so the LORD has compassion on those who fear him" (Psalm 103:13). God shows us compassion as his children. To teach our children mercy, we must show them compassion.

On the one hand, who wouldn't want to be compassionate toward their child? On the other hand, who wouldn't be concerned that they are being too easy on their child and perhaps not preparing them for the real world? We have to discover a way to show compassion without leading them to believe there are no consequences for bad decisions. Luke tells us how to do this: "You must be compassionate, just as your Father is compassionate" (Luke 6:36 NLT). God is compassionate, yet he does not allow us to escape the natural consequences of our sins. He continues to discipline us for our growth. Sometimes we're tempted to think that compassion is taking the road of doing nothing—of just pretending everything is OK. Just the opposite, true compassion is the hard work of being patient with another's faults and forgiving their sins, while at the same time encouraging their continued growth and change. Encouragement that endures—that's compassion.

There are many ways to express compassion: the way you listen, the understanding you give, or even a comforting hug. Based on what God reveals about his compassion toward us, here are five specific ways you can show compassion to your children this week:

## 1. Give them hope.

There is an awesome power in hope. Putting my hope in God dramatically shifts my perspective and my values. Without hope, I have to live for what I can get now; with hope, I can live for the future that God has prepared. Without hope, I focus on myself; with hope, the focus shifts to the love of God.

It can be a struggle to give hope to someone who is hurting. Words we intend to be life giving can often sound trite or cliché. A friend has endured a major loss in their business, and you tell them that God can use even this in his plan for their life. As true as your words are, they can sound as though you're just giving a quick answer to a deep need. The same can happen with your child. Suppose she has just suffered the major disappointment of a good friend rejecting her. How do you give hope in a way that doesn't sound like a quick Band-Aid for a boo-boo?

One secret is to speak personally and not prescriptively.

You're not a doctor handing out a dose of hope; you are a fellow believer who has found the joy of hope in the Lord. As a teacher who can happily come up with a quick truth for many situations, I've had to struggle to learn this lesson. Compassion is more than just giving someone the correct Bible answer to their circumstance, and it is also more than holding someone close in hopeless grief. Hope comes to us when we hear how the truth of God's presence and power has become clear even through the pain of someone else's life. This is one of the great gifts we can give to our children. When a friend rejects them, instead of saying, "Jesus will *always* be your friend," and patting them on the head, we can sit down with them and talk about how the genuine love of Jesus has helped us through some of our greatest losses.

## 2. Give them patience.

God is so patient with us! He knows how dramatically better our lives would be if only we would let go of this or that particularly stubborn habit, yet he patiently waits for us to change. This kind of patience is more than just being forced to wait. It is actively choosing to give someone time to change, even when you are certain of their need for change and would rather try to force that change.

God is patient with us because he knows how he designed us, and he knows that patience is the path to transformation of the heart. If you have a problem with saying negative things to others, God could have decided that every time you say a negative word, your tongue would go numb. You might be motivated to change your outer speech, but you might also find a wedge of bitterness being driven into your heart. Because God is after our hearts, he shows us patient love.

You are after your child's heart. Parenting is more than getting kids to follow a prescribed set of actions—you can program a robot to do that. You're not programming your children for obedience; you are part of God's plan for growing them toward Christlikeness. This is why you show them the compassion of patience. You love it when God is patient with you, and therefore you show the same patience to your kids. Patience is not permissiveness. There are many times when you will act quickly to protect your children when they are in danger or to discipline them when they have disobeyed. Patience is recognizing that even as you act quickly in these situations, you act in ways that give their hearts time to change.

We face this reality when we ask one child to apologize to another. We've all been there. We ask him to apologize, and he casts his eyes downward and spits out a "sorry" that sounds more angry than apologetic. Our next statement is often, "Now say it like you mean it." I've done this; maybe you have too—but wait a minute. How can he say it like he means it unless his heart has changed? When we insist that a child whose heart is still angry apologize with loving tenderness in his tone, we're putting him in a place where he has to either lie or disobey us. What is needed is the compassion of patience—maybe letting him spend some time alone in his room so that the anger can dissolve before he offers his apology. Honestly, I find it very difficult to apologize to my wife in the heat of an argument even if I'm getting a sneaking suspicion that she might be right—I need some time to calm down first. I don't want to force my child to do something relationally that even as an adult I'm not able to do!

## 3. Give them a fresh start.

Everyone needs a fresh start at times—a do-over. Sometimes the most powerful thing you can do is say, "We're going to wipe the slate clean. Everything from here on will be a new day."

One of Jesus' best-known stories is about a father and a son and a fresh start. As an exercise for your soul, take a moment to read it right now. Even if you've heard the story many times before, as you read it now, think about all that happens from the perspective of a parent:

> A man had two sons. The younger son told his father, "I want my share of your estate now instead of waiting until you die." So his father agreed to divide his wealth between his sons.
>
> A few days later this younger son packed all his belongings and took a trip to a distant land, and there he wasted all his money on wild living. About the time his money ran out, a great famine swept over the land, and he began to starve. He persuaded a local farmer to hire him to feed his pigs. The boy became so hungry that even the pods he was feeding the pigs looked good to him. But no one gave him anything.
>
> When he finally came to his senses, he said to himself, "At home even the hired men have food enough to spare, and here I am, dying of hunger! I will go home to my father and say, 'Father, I have sinned against both heaven and you, and I am no longer worthy of being called your son. Please take me on as a hired man.'"
>
> So he returned home to his father. And while he was still a long distance away, his father saw him coming. Filled with love and compassion, he ran to his son, embraced him, and kissed him. His son said to him,

"Father, I have sinned against both heaven and you, and I am no longer worthy of being called your son."

But his father said to the servants, "Quick! Bring the finest robe in the house and put it on him. Get a ring for his finger, and sandals for his feet. And kill the calf we have been fattening in the pen. We must celebrate with a feast, for this son of mine was dead and has now returned to life. He was lost, but now he is found." So the party began.

LUKE 15:11–24 NLT

The picture of this father who runs to greet and embrace this son who was lost strikes a strong chord in our emotions. You can even see here a detailed plan for how to give someone a fresh start. The father puts a robe on his back, a ring on his finger, and sandals on his feet, and he cooks a calf for a feast.

The *robe* is a sign of dignity and honor. When you give someone a fresh start, you give them your honor again. The *ring* was used in financial transactions as a seal and therefore was a sign of authority. When you give someone a fresh start, you give them your trust again. You may not, and probably should not, trust them with everything, but you can trust them with something. The *sandals* were a sign of being a son and not a servant, because the servants in the household didn't wear sandals. The son did not have to earn his way back into the family by being a servant; he was immediately accepted back because of the father's grace. When you give someone a fresh start, you give them your acceptance. Finally, the father celebrates the return of the son with a *feast*. When you give someone a fresh start, it always comes with a spirit of celebration. Instead of killing the fattened calf, you might go out for a dish of nonfat yogurt! This celebration is a sign of your belief that the fresh start has real meaning.

## 4. Give them your understanding.

It's easy for us to minimize the hurts of childhood. We are quite sure that the tragedy of a slip on the kindergarten playground or a slight from a seventh-grade friend won't even be remembered in a few months. Yet at that moment it is the most important thing in our child's world. We tell them to "stop that silly crying" over a piece of dropped candy, while at the same time we are swearing at the driver who keeps us from making the green light. I'm glad God gives us his understanding, even though he knows with absolute clarity that the hurts of this world will be forgotten the moment we enter the gates of heaven. When you take time to remember what it's like to be a child, you are showing real compassion.

Remember the second son in Jesus' story of the prodigal? The prodigal son needed a fresh start, but this older son needed his father's compassionate understanding.

> Meanwhile, the older son was in the fields working. When he returned home, he heard music and dancing in the house, and he asked one of the servants what was going on. "Your brother is back," he was told, "and your father has killed the calf we were fattening and has prepared a great feast. We are celebrating because of his safe return."
>
> The older brother was angry and wouldn't go in. His father came out and begged him, but he replied, "All these years I've worked hard for you and never once refused to do a single thing you told me to. And in all that time you never gave me even one young goat for a

feast with my friends. Yet when this son of yours comes back after squandering your money on prostitutes, you celebrate by killing the finest calf we have."

His father said to him, "Look, dear son, you and I are very close, and everything I have is yours. We had to celebrate this happy day. For your brother was dead and has come back to life! He was lost, but now he is found!"

LUKE 15:25–32 NLT

What I love about this story is that the father went out to find the older brother, and even after the son refused to listen, the father continued to speak words of understanding. In the culture of Jesus' day, the oldest son was expected to be a host at a family celebration, and therefore his absence was a public insult to his father. The father had every right to be angry. Yet he shows compassion by telling his son that he still trusts him with the family inheritance and by explaining to him why he is celebrating.

Compassionate understanding is not always expressed with words. It often comes through physical expression. A gentle and affirming hug often has more power to show compassion to a child who is feeling alone than the speaking of a thousand words.

As we offer understanding, we often have the greatest difficulty when our children struggle with the same things we struggle with. You know how much your impatience has cost you at times, so when you see it in your children, you feel your own frustration and even some anxiety that you may have passed this impatience along to them. The good news is, you have the opportunity to show them a life-changing compassion as you share from the perspective of someone who has been through the same kind of struggle.

## 5. Give them your forgiveness.

Some think the most challenging verses in the Bible are those we struggle to understand. Not so for me. I'm much more challenged by the verses I clearly understand yet have a difficult time putting into practice. One such verse is Ephesians 4:32: "Be kind and compassionate to one another, forgiving each other, just as in Christ God forgave you." Could God be any clearer? God forgave me, so I am to forgive others.

Perhaps no one can hurt us as deeply as our children. When they lie to us or shut us out or stubbornly disobey, the hurt that goes to the deepest part of our souls is often beyond words. Something in us knows that children just should not treat parents that way. It's easy to feel a justification—a rightness in our souls—when we refuse to forgive a child until they adequately and completely ask for our forgiveness. The truth is, we must forgive everyone the same way: instantly and completely. We need to see lack of forgiveness as radioactive waste to our souls—something we need to deal with immediately! The longer we struggle to forgive, the more the bitterness grows. Bitterness creates barriers in relationships, and we can easily reach a point where our refusal to forgive is an even greater enemy of the relationship than the original offense. Rarely will any of us feel like forgiving, but when we look at the forgiveness Jesus has given us, it will give us the power to forgive. I know many parents who have discovered a new sense of freedom and joy in their lives as they've made the choice to pray this simple prayer: "Lord, I forgive my child."

As we look back at these five ways to express compassion, it's significant that both the Old Testament Hebrew word and the New Testament Greek word for *compassion* grow out of the idea of caring for someone with the strength of your inner organs. People in Old Testament times thought of the bowels as the center of the emotions, and in New Testament times, the heart or lungs. The meaning is the same. Compassion is loving someone from the inside out. It can come only when you put yourself in someone else's shoes. The more you view their struggle, hurt, or pain from their perspective, the more compassionate you can be.

Compassion is being like Jesus: "When he saw the crowds, he had compassion on them, because they were harassed and helpless, like sheep without a shepherd" (Matthew 9:36). Jesus saw that people were stressed and that they didn't know where to go to get help—and compassion flowed from him. Don't try to be compassionate on just your own strength of emotion; you'll wear out. Ask the compassionate Christ to empower you to give a compassion beyond yourself to your children.

### Response from the Heart of a Mom

*Hope, patience, fresh starts, understanding, forgiveness. This puts words around what it means for me to be compassionate like God is compassionate. There is such a tension in parenting between discipline and compassion. When my children fail to do the chores I've asked them to do, I have to remember that it's not just one or the other. I can discipline with compassion. The tension seems to melt away and the choice becomes clear when I approach parenting the way that God parents me—showing tender compassion, understanding, and forgiveness while still allowing me to experience the consequences of my choices.*

WEEK 4, DAY 19: **The Gift of Compassion**

- **Verse to remember:** "You must be compassionate, just as your Father is compassionate" (Luke 6:36 NLT).

- **Action to take:** Ask yourself if there is a specific way you can show compassion to your child today —by giving them hope or patience or a fresh start or understanding or forgiveness.

- **Tomorrow:** Forgiveness unlocks families.

# Forgiveness
# Unlocks Families

One of the greatest lessons we can teach our children is how to forgive.

Earlier we looked at the family of Jacob—a family that had to learn to forgive. When ten brothers sell their younger brother into slavery and lie to their father, telling him that he was killed, there is certainly a family that needs to forgive.

Genesis 43 is an insightful look at what happens to a family when someone has been wronged and a deep resentment lives within its four walls. In Jacob's family, the wrong had been done within the family itself. However, whether the cause of a deep-seated unforgiveness comes from inside or outside the family, the result is the same. Everyone begins to play predictable parts in this family system now poisoned by unforgiveness.

Jacob's family is in trouble because of the decisions they've made, and we see them playing all the parts a family plays when faced with an unspoken need to forgive. As we look at the different roles played by those in this family, I invite you to take an honest look at your own family

—both your family now and the family you grew up in. My hope is that if you experience a realization that you may have been caught up in unhealthy patterns, you will also see that God provides for your family right now the promise of redemption and change. We'll take a look at the parts played by members of this family that, by God's grace, ultimately escaped this dysfunction of unforgiveness: Jacob, Judah, nine of the brothers, Benjamin, and Joseph.

***Jacob—the defeated skeptic.*** Remember that Jacob's son Joseph is now the governor of Egypt, but Jacob thinks he has died, and the brothers have no idea that it was Joseph they had met with when they went to Egypt to get food because of a worldwide famine. Joseph had asked for the brothers to bring back their youngest brother, Benjamin, when they returned for more food. Jacob doesn't trust these brothers to take the boy with them, but he knows they must have food. He says, "Take your brother also and go back to the man at once. And may God Almighty grant you mercy before the man so that he will let your other brother and Benjamin come back with you. As for me, if I am bereaved, I am bereaved" (Genesis 43:13–14).

Jacob has descended to the place of a defeated skeptic in his thinking, trapped between facing his family's starvation and the necessity of sending his youngest to get food, sure of his death. Jacob says, "If I am bereaved, I am bereaved." This deep sense of powerlessness, of not being able to do anything while being sure another tragedy is around the next corner—that's the defeated skeptic. Often we see this in the oldest in the family. Instead of leading your family to hope, you feel as though life has kicked all of the hope right out of you.

***Judah—the responsible martyr.*** Judah, one of the older

brothers in this family of twelve boys, suggests a plan to his father, Jacob:

> "Send the boy along with me and we will go at once, so that we and you and our children may live and not die. I myself will guarantee his safety; you can hold me personally responsible for him. If I do not bring him back to you and set him here before you, I will bear the blame before you all my life. As it is, if we had not delayed, we could have gone and returned twice."
>
> GENESIS 43:8–10

Judah convinces his father to send Benjamin along by promising to "bear the blame ... all my life." This may sound like Judah is the only one who has it right, until you realize he has yet to be honest about the blame he bears for selling Joseph into slavery more than twenty years earlier. Most families have a responsible martyr like Judah, someone who says, "I'll take the blame. My shoulders are broad; put it all on me." But if the problem is someone else's responsibility or if they make grand statements without admitting past failings, this martyr complex is really just another piece of a broken family.

*The brothers—the innocent bystanders.* Aside from a few comments from Reuben, the other brothers don't say much. They act the part of innocent bystanders. They are far from innocent, of course. Every one of them except Benjamin was there when Joseph was sold into slavery; each of them is keeping this terrible secret from their father. But over the years they likely had come to determine that it wasn't really so much *their* fault; Joseph had brought it on himself because of his selfish pride. The attitude of "innocent bystander" is perfectly revealed when Jacob asks the brothers why they told Joseph that their younger brother, Benjamin, was not with them on the first trip to Egypt for food.

> They replied, "The man questioned us closely about ourselves and our family. 'Is your father still living?' he asked us. 'Do you have another brother?' We simply answered his questions. How were we to know he would say, 'Bring your brother down here'?"
>
> GENESIS 43:7

*How were we to know? It's not our fault. We're just a victim of these circumstances that are outside of our control.*

***Benjamin—the sacrificial lamb.*** It is decided that Benjamin will go with the brothers to get food from Joseph in Egypt. "So the men took the gifts and double the amount of silver, and Benjamin also. They hurried down to Egypt and presented themselves to Joseph" (Genesis 43:15). The significant truth is that even though the entire chapter is about whether they will take this brother along, Benjamin himself never gets to say a word. There is at least one Benjamin in every family that has been broken by unforgiveness. Often the youngest or the weakest, they are constantly put in places of physical and emotional danger in order to "protect the family." Whether through being cut off from normal relationships with friends to support a dysfunctional family or leaving the home at an early age without the safety of a parent's care, they've become the sacrificial lamb for the family. If you were put in this terrible position in your childhood, it's crucial that you talk with someone you trust about how to come to terms with what you faced.

***Joseph—the one who holds the keys to change.*** When a family is broken because of a family member who needs to forgive, the keys to change are held by the one needing to forgive. Of course, each person in the family can move on in a healthy way without that person letting go of their longtime resentment. But in order for the family as a whole to be healed, for there to be a sense of release and renewal in family interactions and conversations, forgiveness must happen. The one holding on to bitterness is the one who can release the family by forgiving.

Joseph did not immediately express forgiveness to his family, who had hurt him deeply. In fact, instead of forgiving them, he tests them. He gives the youngest brother, Benjamin, greater portions of food at a meal to see if the others will be jealous, and he even plants false evidence against Benjamin to see if the others will abandon him. He tests them to see if he can trust them.

The truth is, you do not have to trust someone before you can forgive them. Yes, you must trust them before you can allow them back into your life in a way that they might be able to say or do something that would hurt you again. But this is different from forgiveness. Restoration and forgiveness are two separate things. Forgiveness can be immediate; restoration takes time, and it involves the rebuilding of trust. The good news is, you can trust God and forgive right now. You may be holding your entire family in a prison by refusing to forgive. This isn't just about you; it's affecting every person whom you love. The other person has a responsibility to rebuild trust if the relationship is to be restored, but you have a responsibility to forgive so that your unforgiveness doesn't damage every other relationship in your family.

A few chapters back, we were reminded that great parents need to know they are forgiven. But it doesn't stop here. Great parents also need to be empowered to forgive others. You can do everything else right for your children, and yet a deeply held resentment can seep into their lives in horrifying ways. To those closest to you, holding resentment in your heart is like building your home on a toxic waste dump.

It's important to wake up to what's been happening in your family, and it's just as important to know you'll never be motivated to forgive by feelings of guilt over what might happen to your family if you do not forgive. Guilt cannot motivate forgiveness; only God's love can do that. When you realize how much he has forgiven you, you receive the strength to forgive others.

Over these five days of looking at what it means to show and teach mercy, we have tapped the core of what it means to parent with the love of Jesus. As you choose not to exasperate your children and to lovingly discipline them, you are expressing God's love to them in ways they can hear at any age. As you show compassion, they are reminded in some small way of the magnificent compassion of our heavenly Father. And as you give forgiveness when you have been hurt, you are showing them how to do what can be done only by depending on the love and forgiveness of Christ.

### *Response from the Heart of a Mom*

*"You must trust God, and God alone, in order to forgive." This is certainly something I must model for my children. I often don't even realize I'm holding on to unforgiveness. There have been times when my children have been the ones to point out the unforgiveness toward a friend or family member that I was refusing to let go of.*

WEEK 4, DAY 20: **Forgiveness Unlocks Families**

- **Verse to remember:** "So I confessed my sins and told them all to you. I said, 'I'll tell the LORD each one of my sins.' Then you forgave me and took away my guilt" (Psalm 32:5 CEV).

- **Action to take:** Begin by recognizing, accepting, and trusting God's wonderful forgiveness for you given through Christ.

- **Next week:** Parenting Principle #5: Serve your children well.

# Serve Your Children Well

## The Power of Your Serving

[Jesus said,] "Let the senior among you become like the junior; let the leader act the part of the servant.

"Who would you rather be: the one who eats the dinner or the one who serves the dinner? You'd rather eat and be served, right? But I've taken my place among you as the one who serves."

Luke 22:26–27 MSG

# A Great
# Parent

People have many different opinions about the path to greatness; bookstore shelves are filled with ideas. Jesus told us clearly the one ingredient without which greatness can never be achieved in any arena of life: "Whoever wants to become great among you must be your servant, and whoever wants to be first must be your slave—just as the Son of Man did not come to be served, but to serve, and to give his life as a ransom for many" (Matthew 20:26–28).

Jesus turns our thinking upside down and tells us that if we want to be great at anything, we have to be a great servant. To be truly great at our work, we must be a great servant at work; to be great at school, we must be a great servant at school.

Want to be a great parent? Be a great servant to your children! Greatness is in replacing the selfish choice with the servant choice. The longer we are parents, the more we realize that much of the process of parenting is learning to be less selfish—learning to be a servant. Sometimes we feel like home is the one place we can place our servant role on the shelf. We tell ourselves, "I work hard and serve others all day long, so my home is the one place I can reward myself by being a little selfish." Just the opposite is true; it's at home that you are given one of your most important opportunities to be a servant. At first this may sound like a wearying prospect for already tired parents. Actually, taking on the attitude of a servant changes our perspective in profoundly energizing ways—ways we'll be looking at this week. There are thousands of ways to serve our children. Over the next several days, we'll focus on how to serve our children by providing for them, protecting them, leading them to faith, helping them to grow in faith, and praying for them.

The word *servant* is easy to trip on. Jesus is not talking about a condition that is forced on a group of people; that would be slavery, not service. He is talking about a choice that is made by an individual. Reduced to its core, serving means we give up our selfishness in order to meet someone else's need. It takes both giving up selfishness and meeting another's need to be a servant.

If we act out of selfish motives, it's not serving, no matter how altruistic it might look to others. Many who appear to be the most impressive servants are actually motivated more by pride or fear than by unselfish love. To get more personal, many of our acts of service grow more out of a desire to look good to others than a genuine unselfishness. When we jump to help our crying child because we're afraid of what other parents in the restaurant might think of us, there is more of self than service. When we comfort and clean up a child who just threw up in the middle of the night, that's pure service!

Serving is acting unselfishly, and it is acting to meet another's need. When we just do whatever someone else wants us to do, that's more people pleasing than it is serving. Jesus served to meet needs, not to satisfy wants. Even as he argued with those blinded by religious rules, he was serving them, encouraging them through painful words to move toward God's genuine love. We must realize that our greatest service to our children can come through an argument. It would be far easier to just ignore talking with them about the friends they are choosing, but we wade into the conversation fully aware that we are risking conflict. We are not doing what they want or even what we want, yet we are meeting their need. That's serving.

As we begin our focus on serving our children, I start on an encouraging note. There are ways you serve your children that may seem automatic to you, yet these can be extremely powerful for them. Among the most significant are the two ways of serving we'll look at on this first day: (1) how we provide for our children and (2) how we protect our children.

## 1. Serve by providing for your children.

One of God's greatest gifts to us is the way he provides for our daily needs. Psalm 104 is an amazing picture of our Provider, who gives us our daily bread. This means you are performing a sacred act of service when you scrape a piece of burned toast and spread some butter on it for your child to eat before they head off to school. You are passing along the provision of God to meet their need. Do not miss the significance of your serving as you provide a roof over their head, food for their stomach, books for their education, and security for their future.

As we provide for our children, we put things in perspective by teaching them to praise our provider God. We provide for our child's daily needs by giving them food and shelter; we provide for a lifetime of spiritual needs when we teach them to appreciate God for all he gives.

I've come to believe there is one way of appreciating God that has more impact than any other. Of course it is good to praise God for what he has given by praying before a meal or telling stories of how God has provided for your family. But an even more powerful impact results from teaching our children to give back to God. When they decide to give a portion of their hard-earned allowance or paycheck from their first job, that action has a profound influence on their hearts. In fact, as a general rule, the earlier you teach your children to give, the more giving they will be. Children often find it easier to give to God than adults do; because they must depend on their parents, they more easily depend on God. When Chaundel and I taught our children about tithing at a very young age, they didn't ask, "Do we have to give 10 percent?" They asked, "Why can't I give 50 percent?" Children tend to give with attitudes of simple trust and abundant generosity, more aware of their joy of giving than impressed with themselves as givers. These are attitudes that, when begun early in life, have lasting power to permeate the heart that your children have toward God as their provider. Putting this in practical terms, we must help our children to make giving a part of their worship. As much as I value the worship times for children that fit their learning level, one of the things we sometimes miss is providing the opportunity for our children to give to the offering so they can develop this habit of giving. Even if your children's worship program doesn't do this, you can encourage your child to bring an offering and give to God.

## 2. Serve by protecting your children.

God is our protector, so when you are protecting your children, you are serving like God does. Think of the power of these simple acts of service. You bundle your baby against the cold; you refuse to let your child's fingers wiggle free as you cross a busy street; you buckle the child's seat belt in the car for the thousandth time; you take your sick child to the doctor; you stand between your child and danger. When you do these things, you are serving in the most significant of ways. Without many of these acts of service, your children would not survive to adulthood.

Seemingly simple acts of service are often our greatest acts of service. You do not usually do your most significant serving in a single moment of dramatic unselfishness; it is more often carried out in the routine actions of everyday life. Jesus taught us this truth when he washed his disciples' feet (John 13). In Jesus' day, washing feet was not a special religious ceremony. It was done all the time, because peoples' feet were dirty. When everyone else was too caught up in themselves to take time to wash the feet of others, Jesus took up a basin and a towel. After washing his disciples' feet, he said, "I have given you an example to follow. Do as I have done to you" (John 13:15 NLT). He wasn't talking about washing feet so much as about serving to meet practical needs. This is exactly what you can have the heart to do as a parent. You can choose to see beyond the task of changing a diaper or driving in a car pool or tending a scraped knee. You are doing as Jesus did.

## Response from the Heart of a Mom

*Giving up my selfish desires in order to serve my children—that automatically comes with pregnancy for a mom, right? Not a chance. I think we do young moms in particular a huge disservice by subtly sending the message that all women have an inborn bent to take the worst piece of chicken on the plate. I was shocked to realize the many selfish feelings I had toward our children. I have literally caught myself hundreds of times choosing to serve our children—but doing so out of selfish motives. It's encouraging to be reminded of all the ways we serve our children almost automatically throughout each day.*

WEEK 5, DAY 21: **A Great Parent**

- **Verse to remember:** "Whoever wants to become great among you must be your servant, and whoever wants to be first must be your slave—just as the Son of Man did not come to be served, but to serve, and to give his life as a ransom for many" (Matthew 20:26–28).

- **Action to take:** It's easy to miss all that we do as parents. To remind yourself, take a piece of paper and write down some of the ways that you provide for and protect your children on a daily basis.

- **Tomorrow:** Leading toward faith

# Leading
# toward Faith

We're talking this week about practical actions that stem from a servant's heart toward our children. Yesterday we saw the value of providing for and protecting our children. Today we look at the opportunity to serve our children by leading them toward their own relationship with Jesus. John writes, "Yet to all who received [Jesus], to those who believed in his name, he gave the right to become children of God" (John 1:12). Can you imagine anything more fulfilling than helping one of your children become a child of God? You have a role to play as they begin a relationship that will change their eternity.

Throughout the Bible, we can detect a sometimes inconspicuous yet extremely powerful undercurrent of the spiritual influence of parents. John Mark, the writer of the gospel of Mark, was certainly influenced by his mother, Mary. Acts 12:12 tells us the early church met in his mother's home. There is evidence suggesting that the disciples met with Jesus in the home of John Mark's family to eat the Passover the night before his death.

Alexander and Rufus, two brothers who were leaders in

the early church in Rome (Mark 15:21; Romans 16:13), had parents who were a powerful spiritual influence in their lives. We know their father by name, Simon — the man pressed into service to carry Jesus' cross. His life and heart were changed that day, and the dramatic spiritual change impacted his family. We don't know these two boys' mother by name, but we do know she is praised by Paul as someone who had been like a mother to him.

As we look at the lives of people of faith in the Bible, we often see the influence of parents of faith. The mother and grandmother of Timothy, an early leader of the church, gave him the gift of faith as a child. The man in charge of the jail at Philippi was led to faith by his prisoners, Paul and Barnabas, and immediately led his entire family to faith in Jesus as well. When you have a genuine faith, you will naturally influence your children toward genuine faith in their lives.

As important as we know this is, I know it's not always where we live. We struggle with just getting our kids to eat their green beans or do their homework. We get caught up in the everyday challenges of life. Once we lift our eyes beyond the daily reality to the eternal realities, the questions start to come to our minds. There are a couple of big questions I'm often asked about leading children to faith in Jesus. The number one question is, "How do I know when my child is at a point when he is ready to make this kind of commitment to God?" We think to ourselves, "I don't want to force them. I don't want to push them. I don't want it to be about me. I want it to be *their* decision."

At its core, this is a matter of sensitivity to your child's maturity. You'll often begin to see their readiness to enter a relationship with Christ as you listen to the questions they are asking. Your child may begin to ask more about why things are done in a certain way at church or about what baptism means. One of the main ways you can know is when you see that your child understands that they have done wrong. Jesus Christ came to be our Savior, to save us from the wrong things we do. Obviously a child is going to understand sin on a very different level than an adult does; but when a child gets to the point where they feel sorrow or shame, they're very likely ready. You can't assign an age to this; it's different for all children.

Some of you may have an older child whom you know is ready for faith, yet they have not yet chosen to accept the gift of God's love. You've done all we'll be talking about in this chapter, so then what do you do? I believe God's words to wives with husbands who have not yet believed are also appropriate for parents: "If they refuse to listen when you talk to them about the Lord, they will be won by your respectful, pure behavior. Your godly lives will speak to them better than any words" (1 Peter 3:1 LB).

Keep living the faith, praying with all your heart, and entrusting them to God.

The other big question people ask is, "How do I do this? Do I have to bring them to some kind of class? Are the instructions written down in some book? What exactly do I do to lead them to faith?"

Some parents don't talk to their kids about God because they're afraid their kids will ask a question they can't answer. Let me set your mind at ease. They *will* ask questions you can't answer! This may well give you the best opportunity to teach them. In that moment, you have a choice: you can fake it and use big words to confuse them, or you can say, "I'm learning about God too."

Although you may not be able to answer why God allowed their dog to die or whether God can make a rock so big even he can't lift it, you certainly can answer their questions about beginning a relationship with Jesus. This is the answer that will one day answer every other question! It's really very simple. You just talk to Jesus with them. You say, "Let's tell Jesus you want to have a relationship with him, that you want to ask him to come in and be a part of your life, and that you want to follow him for the rest of your life." In just that simple a prayer, you talk to Jesus with your children.

I'm praying that as you read this, many of you will find that the time is right to talk to Jesus with your child about beginning a relationship with him. I'm praying that God will give some of you an opportunity to do that this week.

With our three children, we wanted to be there when they crossed that line and made a personal commitment to Jesus Christ. Yet our first two kids, Ryan and Alyssa, made this commitment when we weren't there. Ryan prayed alone at home. Alyssa walked out of her room one day and said, "Guess what? I just gave my life to Jesus Christ. I just wanted you to know." We rejoiced with her, but we were also thinking, "We wanted to be there! Couldn't you have called us in to listen?"

Since we weren't there with the first two kids, we watched the spiritual readiness of our youngest like a hawk! If at all possible, we were going to be there with Luke. One day the opportunity came. He had been arguing with his little friend Kelsey about what it meant to be a Christian. He had said it meant to do good things in your life for God. She said, "No, Luke. It means you have a relationship with Jesus, and that's why you do the good things." Luke was looking for us to support his side in the argument. We said, "Luke, actually Kelsey is right. It *is* a relationship with Jesus. This is where it starts." Then we sat down on the floor with Luke and had the opportunity to talk with him and pray with him as he asked Jesus Christ into his life.

What a privilege! I pray that you'll have this privilege. I also pray the next thing that happened to us doesn't happen to you. About two hours later, as we ate lunch, Luke looked at us and said, "I don't want to be a Christian anymore." I thought, "Oh no! It lasted only two hours. And I'm a pastor!" I said, "Luke, why don't you want to be a Christian?" He said, "If I'm a Christian, it means I have to admit that Kelsey was right and I was wrong. So I don't want to be a Christian anymore." So he became a man on the same day that he became a Christian! We talked it through, of course, and Luke quickly became OK with his newfound faith.

Once your child has made this commitment, you celebrate. One of the great tasks of parenting is celebrating. Celebrate everything—from the first bites of solid food and successes in potty training to the last days of high school and achievements in a new job. The celebrations of a mom and dad are significant to the core of a child's soul. Amid the more obvious celebrations of a good report card or a game-winning soccer goal, don't miss the opportunities to celebrate their faith. Jesus said, "There will be more rejoicing in heaven over one sinner who repents than over ninety-nine righteous persons who do not need to repent" (Luke 15:7). Think of the power of a Father in heaven and parents on earth rejoicing together in the new faith of a child! This is one of the most important, and most wonderful, ways you can serve!

*Response from the Heart of a Mom*

*Oh, what wonderful, tender, and poignant memories I have about our kids' decisions to receive Christ! What joy to know from their birth that the God who created them would also welcome them into a relationship with himself when they asked! My mind also turns to a mother who was spiritually sensitive to her daughter's probing questions and led me to experience a very real faith of my own at a young age.*

WEEK 5, DAY 22: **Leading toward Faith**

- **Verse to remember:** "Yet to all who received him, to those who believed in his name, he gave the right to become children of God" (John 1:12).

- **Action to take:** Pray about and plan for a time when you can talk with your child, who may be ready to offer a prayer asking for forgiveness and expressing trust in Jesus.

- **Tomorrow:** Prayers that last a lifetime

# Prayers That Last a Lifetime

As we look this week at the path to great parenting through serving, I can think of no greater way to serve our children than by praying for them. Consider the truth for parents contained in these familiar verses about prayer:

> In the same way, the Spirit helps us in our weakness. We do not know what we ought to pray for, but the Spirit himself intercedes for us with groans that words cannot express.
>
> ROMANS 8:26

> So we have continued praying for you ever since we first heard about you. We ask God to give you a complete understanding of what he wants to do in your lives, and we ask him to make you wise with spiritual wisdom.
>
> COLOSSIANS 1:9 NLT

> "My prayer is not that you take them out of the world but that you protect them from the evil one."
>
> JOHN 17:15

"As for me, far be it from me that I should sin against the LORD by failing to pray for you. And I will teach you the way that is good and right."

1 SAMUEL 12:23

This last verse is convicting because I know I have often sinned by failing to pray. How is it a sin not to pray? The Bible says that whatever I do that is not from faith is sin (Romans 14:23). When I fail to pray, it is often an indication that I'm depending on my own power, not God's power. Not necessarily because I intend to. Sometimes it's just because I forget. I don't take the time to focus on him.

There's something powerful about prayer that can change everything. Chaundel tells this story about being encouraged to pray:

I'll never forget how Ryan encouraged me in how important it is to pray for our kids. He was just starting college, and we were going through all the emotions of seeing our first child go away. Tom, Ryan, and I drove to Chicago in the car Ryan would have at college. It was an enjoyable trip but one containing an underlying tension about our pending separation. Before we left him, being a mom who wanted to do something to help, I asked, "So, Ryan, what can I most do for you? What do you want? Do you want cookies? Do you want Post-it Notes? What do you most want from me?" He said, "Mom, I just want you to pray for me." Oh! It was hard. I wanted to *do* something. He said, "The best thing you can do is pray for me."

I had been reading 1 Samuel in my quiet time. Tom and I had struggled through years of infertility and thought we weren't going to be able to have children when we were a young married couple, so the story of Hannah waiting for Samuel's birth has always been special to me. Her words from 1 Samuel 1:27–28 had hung above Ryan's bed: "For this child I prayed ... and now I've dedicated him to the Lord." I was going back over these verses and recommitting him to the Lord, trying to let go and let go and let go.

And then I got to the verse in chapter 12 that reads, "Far be it from me that I should sin against the LORD by failing to pray for you" (1 Samuel 12:23). God used this verse to make it abundantly clear that prayer is one of my greatest actions—and one of my greatest privileges —as a parent.

I must keep coming back to this truth. There have been so many times, not only with Ryan, but with Alyssa and Luke, when I've asked in my mind, "What do they most need from me?"

As parents, when and how should we pray? As much as we want to pray, we tend to get caught up in the busyness of the day and miss the opportunity to talk to our Father about our children. The answers to these questions are as unique as we are. Prayer is talking to God relationally, and so every one of us will pray and be motivated to pray in different ways. If you're talking to a friend in a way that doesn't fit you, the conversation will sound strained and unnatural. The same is true of your conversation with God. Whenever you feel you must pray like someone else, using their methods and timing, you'll feel like you're in a suit that just doesn't fit. When something doesn't fit, we tend to leave it hanging on the rack.

With this uniqueness in mind, there is no doubt we can learn from each other in prayer. Here are several ideas that have encouraged parents to pray for their children. I can guarantee you not every one of them will fit you. Try each one on until you find one or two you can modify to work best for you.

**1. *Use a prayer and thanksgiving journal.*** Record your prayers for your children in the journal, both your requests and your thanksgiving to God. It helps to approach your prayers with more than just an immediate need in mind. For example, you can pray for God's work in growing your child in the four areas we talked about on day three of our first week: physically, intellectually, socially, and spiritually.

**2. *Pray throughout the day.*** Prayer cannot be limited to a list we try to pray through at the beginning of the day. Too often, the day starts with an immediate need, and then we never get to the list. It can be helpful to pray according to your children's schedule, talking to God about where they are right at that moment. When they are preschoolers, ask God to use their scheduled naps and playtimes to help them grow; when they are in elementary school, pray for their learning times and their recesses; when they are in middle school, ask God to help them learn as they are in their math or English class. These prayers throughout the day may often be no more than a few seconds of conversation with God.

**3. *Use triggers as reminders.*** It can be helpful to set up triggers, things you see throughout the day that remind you to pray. When you open a door or start the car or end a meeting, you can remind yourself to pray for your children for a few minutes. Some parents are helped by intentional triggers, such as wearing a wristband that reminds them to pray every time they see it.

**4. *Get together with others to pray.*** There is no doubt the best reminder to pray comes through the mutual accountability of meeting with others. In your home or at your work, you could meet once a week with a few others with the express intention of praying for your children. If your schedule doesn't allow you to meet, you could find a friend who agrees to pray with you and receive text messages of your prayers for your children as you pray them. For those of us who are frustrated that we don't pray for our children enough, the secret to change can be finding another person who will be a mutual encourager in prayer.

**5. *Pray Bible verses.*** Sometimes we stop praying because it seems we've prayed the same thing so many times. We know God is interested, but somehow we've lost a sense of the fresh conversation of prayer. When that happens, it can be helpful to pray Bible verses. This is true in any area of our prayer, and especially so as parents. When you pray the truth of God's Word for your children, you can be certain you're praying exactly in God's will for them. Here's a verse you can pray for your kids today: "We ask God to give you a complete understanding of what he wants to do in your lives, and we ask him to make you wise with spiritual wisdom" (Colossians 1:9 NLT).

As you serve your children by praying for them, don't miss the power in that seemingly simple moment. The power of a praying parent is an awesome thing. The prayers you pray for your kids are going to be answered all their lives, even after you've been in heaven for many years.

### Response from the Heart of a Mom

*Being faithful in prayer for our children (and grand-children!) is still a struggle for me. I appreciate all the tips Tom has shared and agree that you have to find what works for you. For years I used a daily list of thirty character qualities with verses to pray for each of our kids. With Alyssa having been in Rwanda for several years now, I have a reminder on my calendar to send her the verse I'm praying for her for this coming week. I haven't been as consistent as I would like, but it helps my focus in prayer for her.*

WEEK 5, DAY 23: **Prayers That Last a Lifetime**

- **Verse to remember:** "As for me, far be it from me that I should sin against the Lord by failing to pray for you. And I will teach you the way that is good and right" (1 Samuel 12:23).

- **Action to take:** Stop and offer a brief prayer for each of your children right now.

- **Tomorrow:** Encouraging spiritual growth

# Encouraging Spiritual Growth

You cannot cause your child to grow physically; only God can do that. But you can encourage the growth that God is causing by providing good nutrition, ensuring that they get adequate rest, and caring for them when they are sick. This same principle is true when it comes to their spiritual growth. You cannot cause growth, but you can encourage growth.

God specifically directs us to serve our children by encouraging their spiritual growth: "Bring them up in the training and instruction of the Lord" (Ephesians 6:4). The Greek word for "bring them up" means to "nourish up to maturity." What a great picture! It's like nurturing a plant; you cannot cause the plant to grow or to produce fruit, but the way you water and fertilize the plant has everything to do with how well it grows. We have a wonderful part to play in the growth of our children.

One of the most powerful expressions of our responsibility for others' growth is found in Galatians 4:19: "I am again in the pains of childbirth until Christ is formed in you." This verse points us to the goal we are reaching toward in spiritual growth: Christ being formed in us. It is the goal of being like Jesus in our character and in our actions. These words remind us that God is doing the work, not us. He is the one who is doing the forming, even as a potter at a wheel forms the clay with a gentle touch of his hands.

This verse also pictures the powerful influence we can have on another's growth, using the phrase "the pains of childbirth." A mother does not create the baby that is inside her, but she is definitely involved in bringing this baby into the world! It is with labor—hard work, painful work—that a child is brought into this world; and it is with labor that we work for the spiritual growth of our children. We have many partners in this growth. Words cannot express how deeply grateful we are for the children's and student ministries at Saddleback Church, which have invested so greatly in the lives of all three of our children. You never want to labor alone for the growth of your children, yet as a parent you know there will never be anyone who has a greater responsibility to labor for them than you.

Let's get practical. How do we labor for real-world growth in our children? How do we labor in ways that help rather than hinder their growth? We've all seen circumstances where a lot of effort went into a child's spiritual training, yet the child ended up being pushed away from God.

The secret to healthy growth is *balance*. This is true physically; it takes balanced nutrition and exercise to grow a strong body. It is true intellectually; the mind best develops through balanced learning across several disciplines by means of a mix of methods. It is also true spiritually; we grow stronger by balancing God's purposes of fellowship, discipleship, worship, ministry, and evangelism in our lives.

We have the privilege of helping our children learn to balance God's purposes. The five purposes of God that we can read about in Rick Warren's book *The Purpose Driven Life* are not for adults only! The earlier we begin to learn and balance these purposes, the healthier our growth will be.

Above all others, you have the opportunity to strengthen your children's relationship with God as you teach them these five things:

## 1. How to be a *member* of God's family.

Just think about how the early lessons we teach our children grow into life lessons about how we treat one another in God's family! When you teach your toddler not to bite another child in the nursery, you're paving a path for them not to be backbiting as adults. When you talk to your children about how to handle their negative attitudes toward a child who said something negative to them in Sunday school, you're teaching them how not to be a gossip in later life. When you come up with an idea together for how to help a child who is hurting over a loss, you're showing your child how to minister to the body of Christ for the rest of their life.

At the same time, we know that our children also learn from our *bad* examples. If they see your jealous attitude toward a fellow believer, there's a good chance they'll repeat that pattern in later life. Ouch! That one hurts, because none of us are perfect in relationships or with our words. So when we mess up, we have the chance to fess up—knowing how much they'll learn from an honest confession like, "No matter how hurt I was, I just shouldn't have spoken that way about them."

## 2. How to *mature* in their faith.

One of the great gifts we can give our children for their personal growth is the development of habits. As we model habits of maturity in our lives and encourage them in our child's life, we are setting patterns that will last a lifetime. In the end, my identity is simply the sum total of my habits. If I have a habit of golfing every Saturday, I'm identified as a golfer. If I have a habit of working in my yard much of every weekend, my identity bears the mark of being a gardener. When we are serious about spending time with Jesus, it expresses our identity as a Christian.

I encourage you to help your children develop habits especially in the ways they deal with their time, their money, and their relationships—because these three areas cover much of our lives. Encourage the habits of spending time with Jesus regularly, giving regularly, and being in a small group of other believers regularly. Just a word on this last one as your children head toward middle school: one of the most important contributions to the spiritual growth of our children came through the small groups they were in during those years. Having a group of peers to meet with during those awkward yet powerfully identity-forming years is immeasurably important. At the very stage of life when we most want to hold on to them, we most need to be releasing them to the added influence of the right leaders and friends.

## 3. How to *minister* to others.

There are two main ways you can encourage your children in the purpose of ministry. The first is *hospitality*—opening your home in order to meet people's needs. Hospitality can mean having fellowship with people from church, having someone come to stay with you after a crisis, making your home a place where lonely people feel welcome, or inviting those who don't know Christ to come for dinner. It can also mean showing hospitality to your children's friends. Since we lived close to the high school, we loved having "Quesadilla Wednesday" for up to fifty hungry teenagers every week. Yes, it was a lot of frenetic effort for their hour-long lunch break, but how could we stop when we heard kids say, "This is my favorite part of the week"? You never know what seemingly small act of service will grow bigger than you hoped and have a greater impact than you could have imagined.

Along with hospitality, you also do *ministry* — going out from your home to meet people's needs. You can go as a family to a Christian training project; you can let your children see you and your spouse serve together at a food kitchen; or you can make something to give to shut-ins.

As your children serve others, they may face failures along the way. We *hate* for our children to be disappointed, yet in protecting them from possible disappointment, we can actually stunt their spiritual growth. As you well know, disappointment is one of the main tools God uses to cause us to grow. When protecting your kids from failure becomes the greater goal, you may find yourself discouraging your child from taking risks unless you're sure of success. Yet these very risks may be vital to their growth.

## 4. How to have a *mission* in the world.

"Mission" means I expand my vision beyond my world. Jesus talked about going to Jerusalem, Judea, and the remotest part of the earth. Ministry differs from mission in that when you take on a mission, you get outside of your world. For a preschooler, the remotest part of the earth could be making cookies to take up the block to a new neighbor. I remember taking our young children with us to an ordination for Spanish pastors in our area where they were able to hear praise and teaching in a different language. You cannot have a mission to the world if you are afraid to go into the world, and taking your children on trips to places that extend their vision will build a confidence God can use in wonderful ways.

I must warn you that this doesn't come without some pain. Our daughter, Alyssa, went with us on a mission trip to Rwanda at age eighteen, and after graduating from college, she is now serving in Rwanda. Would we rather have her closer to us? Of course! Do we have an even deeper joy that she has a mission in the world? Absolutely. (But if you're reading this, Alyssa, we still want you to come home for Christmas!)

## 5. How to *magnify* God.

Worship is more than singing in church. That is one aspect of worship, and it is something we can experience together as families. Just don't think that to teach your kids to worship, you have to learn to play the piano and have a gospel music sing-along every Tuesday night. This may be your dream—believe me, it is not your child's dream!

Worship is recognizing God's worth and worthiness. One of the greatest ways we learn worship in families is through the ups and downs of life. Focus on God, trust him, and praise him when the circumstances in your family are wonderful. "I will praise you, O LORD, with all my heart; I will tell of all your wonders" (Psalm 9:1).

And focus on God, trust him, and even praise him when the troubled times come. "LORD, you are my strength and fortress, my refuge in the day of trouble!" (Jeremiah 16:19 NLT). You don't praise him for the troubles; you praise him that he is powerfully at work, no matter what the trouble — and even through the trouble.

As you encourage your child in these five purposes of God, you are serving them by building their spiritual growth. The Bible often uses the picture of building when referring to our spiritual growth — building not on the sand but on the rock, building a tower, building on a foundation, building each other up (Matthew 7:24–27; Luke 14:28; 1 Corinthians 3:10–11; Ephesians 4:11–13). By serving your children and building into their spiritual growth, you are involving yourself in the greatest construction project on earth!

### Response from the Heart of a Mom

*It's vitally important for us to think about all we need to teach our children. But as a mother, I would quickly become overwhelmed by even just everything I needed to teach them spiritually — much less teaching them to brush their teeth and not pick their nose. Very early I gave myself grace by focusing on this: all I really have to teach my children is to have their own relationship with God, to connect with him on a daily basis. Yes, we did all the other stuff too, but it's really just gravy. If we teach them to make spending time with God a priority even before they can read, then he can teach them the rest!*

WEEK 5, DAY 24: **Encouraging Spiritual Growth**

- **Verse to remember:** "I am again in the pains of childbirth until Christ is formed in you" (Galatians 4:19).

- **Action to take:** Choose one of the five purposes and take a few minutes to think about how you can encourage your child's growth in that purpose.

- **Tomorrow:** Truth along the way

# Truth along the Way

We've talked this week about how to serve our children by providing and protecting, by leading them to faith, by praying for them, and by encouraging their growth. On the last day of this week of reading, we look at one of the most powerful ways to serve our kids: by showing them the truth of God's Word.

Being a parent without knowing the Bible is like trying to fly a 747 without understanding the instrument panel. It's just too complicated a task to accomplish by the seat of your pants. I've known many parents who, as new believers in Christ, were concerned that they didn't know enough of the Bible. When you feel this way, you can make one of two choices: give up because you feel so far behind, or see the opportunity to dig in and learn the Bible with them. You have no idea how valuable this second choice will be to your children. They will be more powerfully influenced by a parent who knows nothing of the Bible yet is deciding to learn than if they had a biblical scholar for a parent who felt they were finished with their learning. Your children need more than a parent who knows God's Word; they need one who is learning God's Word—and each and every parent can do *that*.

Teaching our children God's truth is so important that God gives specific instructions on how to do it:

> Fix these words of mine in your hearts and minds; tie them as symbols on your hands and bind them on your foreheads. Teach them to your children, talking about them when you sit at home and when you walk along the road, when you lie down and when you get up. Write them on the doorframes of your houses and on your gates, so that your days and the days of your children may be many in the land the LORD swore to give your forefathers, as many as the days that the heavens are above the earth.
>
> DEUTERONOMY 11:18–21

These amazing verses reveal many of the learning models we are just clarifying today. Specifically, these verses give us three tasks as we teach Scripture to our children: verbalize God's words, memorize them, and symbolize them.

## 1. Verbalize God's words.

God tells us to talk to our children about his words, and he even tells us when ("when you lie down and when you get up") and where ("when you sit at home and when you walk along the road"). Talk about his Word at different times of the day, realizing that the way we begin and end our day is extremely important, and talk about his Word in different places. There are two powerful learning principles here. First, learning cannot be divorced from life, so we learn God's Word in the midst of life. Children may learn Bible stories and Bible verses and Bible truths in Sunday school, but it is at home that they learn Christlike love and godly attitudes and Christian lifestyles. A child whose family attends church regularly is in church (on average) 1 percent of the time; they are in the home 83 percent of the time.* The second learning principle is that the more places and times we are involved in learning, the better we learn. By learning at different places and times, we learn better and remember it longer. So talk about God's Word throughout the day—at meals, in the car, when your kids get up in the morning, and when they go to bed at night.

One way to do this is by praying for the wisdom to see teachable moments—opportunities to talk about God's Word as children make a decision or face a hurt or enjoy a victory or just go through their day. It can be as simple as praying, "This is the day the LORD has made" (Psalm 118:24) in your prayer at breakfast, or as profound as talking about what it means that "God causes everything to work together for the good of those who love God" (Romans 8:28 NLT) in light of a problem they are having.

Another way we verbalize God's words to our children, especially when they are younger, is by telling stories from the Bible. As our children hear these stories, they learn about the character of God. As you tell about how God divided the Red Sea, they are hearing about God's omnipotence and faithfulness in terms they can begin to grasp. As you talk about Jesus going to the house of Zaccheaus, a man who was hated in his community, they hear about God's kindness, forgiveness, and love.†

---

*Cited in Gary Smalley and Ted Cunningham, *Great Parents, Lousy Lovers: Discover How to Enjoy Life with Your Spouse While Raising Your Kids* (Wheaton, Ill.: Tyndale House, 2010), 136.

†For those of you whose children are preschool age, the four volumes of *Read-Aloud Bible Stories* by Ella Lindvall provide a powerful tool for telling these stories to your children in ways they will remember. For older kids, *The Jesus Storybook Bible* by Sally Lloyd-Jones is loved by many families.

## 2. Memorize God's words.

Children have an amazing ability to memorize. Studies show that instead of memory being a natural ability in children, as is often thought, it is more accurate to say that memorization strengthens their abilities. Memorization is like a core muscle of the mind. It has the power to strengthen our entire structure of thinking. These same studies show that our natural ability to memorize is best when we memorize in the most natural of ways.*

Make memorizing fun. The last thing you want is for your kids to fall out of love with God's Word because all they can remember is the drudgery of memorization. Some parents give rewards; others see how much of a verse they can repeat at a stoplight. Some memorize while on vacation. Many use hand motions, and some put verses to song. Memorization always requires some work, but the more enjoyable we make it, the more we are building our children's love for God's Word.

Encouraging your children to memorize as they enter adolescence becomes more a matter of peer approval. If they are in a group that memorizes verses, they will memorize. Chaundel and I started dating in our senior year of high school and soon decided to memorize verses together. Wanting to impress each other—and being committed to sexual purity—we memorized a lot of verses before we were married! Since our wedding, we haven't done nearly as well at memorizing, which serves as a good reminder to encourage our children to take advantage of the opportunity when it is there.

---

*David Wood, *How Children Think and Learn: The Social Contexts of Cognitive Development* (Oxford: Blackwell, 1988), 77–80.

## 3. Symbolize God's words.

"Tie them as symbols on your hands and bind them on your foreheads," God told Moses. Don't panic, parents; he is not talking about tattoos! They would tie verses to their wrists and in a band around their heads. This translates a little differently today. We wear messages on hats and T-shirts and carry them in our notebooks. Moses told the Israelites to write verses on their doorframes; today we hang them in picture frames. The point it symbolizes is that God's Word is carried with us throughout our day; it serves as a visual declaration that God's Word is part of our household.

It is powerful to have your children get personally involved in these pictures of God's Word throughout your home. The great purveyor of truth in many a home is the refrigerator door! As you put on the door that picture of a Bible story your kids colored in church or an art project based on a Bible verse, you are putting a magnetic stamp of value on their learning of God's words.

As you verbalize, memorize, and symbolize God's words with your children, you are giving them a gift that will last a lifetime. Long after that shiny new bike you gave them for Christmas has turned to rust, these verses will be turning into faith, hope, and love in their minds as adults.

### Response from the Heart of a Mom

*Every parent who has ever helped a child memorize a verse or checked off on their memory assignment knows that God can use this experience powerfully in our lives, as well as those instances when we hear or memorize together God's words. The downside was when our children would quote an appropriate verse to challenge me in a situation!*

*The value of symbolizing God's words was brought home to me as we visited our daughter in Rwanda. We had dropped in on a few families that lived in very basic dwellings on the church property. Undoubtedly some of you have had the experience of being overwhelmed by poverty as you stepped into a little mud hut. I had to fight back tears as I looked up and realized that the only decorations on their walls were the hand-colored Sunday school papers from the previous six or seven weeks of the church's children's program led by our daughter.*

WEEK 5, DAY 25: **Truth along the Way**

- **Verse to remember:** "Fix these words of mine in your hearts and minds; tie them as symbols on your hands and bind them on your foreheads. Teach them to your children, talking about them when you sit at home and when you walk along the road, when you lie down and when you get up. Write them on the doorframes of your houses and on your gates, so that your days and the days of your children may be many in the land the LORD swore to give your forefathers, as many as the days that the heavens are above the earth" (Deuteronomy11:18–21).

- **Action to take:** Try memorizing a verse with your child this week.

- **Next week:** Parenting Principle #6: Live the Golden Rule.

# Live the Golden Rule

## The Power of Your Unselfishness

"Treat others as you want them to treat you."

Luke 6:31 LB

# How Your Kids
# Treat You

In this sixth and last week of looking at parenting, we will boil everything down to the essentials. There are thousands of ideas and opinions about the details of how to raise kids. Some are right for you and your children; some won't work for you. You are an individual; they are individuals—so you have to find things that work for both of you!

As an example of these individual differences in the ways we raise our kids, let's take trying to get your child to eat vegetables. Some say, "Reward them. Tell them that if they eat vegetables, they'll get dessert. Others think, "That'll just turn them into little despots—Napoleon's mom probably rewarded him for eating his green beans." Others use the strategy to wait them out, saying, "We'll just keep sitting at this table until you eat your vegetables." We tried that and realized that our children had more time than we did! It's an idea that will work with some children; others will wait at that table until Jesus comes again and shout on their way to heaven, "Never had to eat those green beans." There are a lot of ideas out there on daily strategies for raising children. Look at them, and find the ones that work best for you.

Looking behind all the strategies, we've been focusing on some of the principles God gives for raising children, principles on which we can build everything. We add now to the principles of love, communication, mercy, and service this teaching of Jesus: "Treat others as you want them to treat you" (Luke 6:31 LB). What is typically called the Golden Rule is a perfect fit for any family, no matter what specific parenting approach you use.

The Golden Rule can only be truly lived out in connection with God. As a human being, I can't always figure out how another person wants or needs to be treated. I can make a good guess based on my own needs, but why not go beyond this to see *what God says* about the meeting of another's needs? God is our creator. He knows and understands us like no one else ever will. And thus there are two questions at the core of parenting: (1) What does God say about how parents are to treat children? and (2) What does God say about how children are to treat parents? We'll begin today with how children are to treat parents; tomorrow we'll look at our responsibility as parents toward our kids.

The Golden Rule finds new and deeper meaning when I understand how God wants my children to treat me. God is crystal clear about the answer; in fact, it's even in the Ten Commandments: "Honor your father and your mother, so that you may live long in the land the LORD your God is giving you" (Exodus 20:12). While there are a hundred good things children can do in relating to their parents, this command tells us there are two essentials: the action of *obedience* and the attitude of *honor*.

In their actions, children are to treat parents with *obe-*

*dience*. "Children, obey your parents as the Lord wants, because this is the right thing to do" (Ephesians 6:1 NCV). Paul says concerning church leaders, "He must have a well-behaved family, with children who obey quickly and quietly" (1 Timothy 3:4 LB). Any parenting technique, book, or system that leaves out obedience is outside of the plan of God. Some may ask, "How can you advocate obedience when it is abused by bad parents?" In the extremely rare case in which parents tragically command an obedience that is torturous or even life threatening, God's command to protect children outweighs the command to obey. It would be an even greater tragedy if we threw out the idea of obedience altogether because of a few pathological parents. It is through obedience to parents that children develop some of the most important skills for daily living. Through obedience, children learn such things as:

- *the discipline of service*. The word *obey* literally means "to hear under." It is the ability to listen and respond to another's direction. I'd say that's an important job skill and life skill! None of us really like it when someone else tells us what to do. Even for us adults, something in us tends to resist another person directing us. It takes discipline to say no to our own selfishness and to follow the direction of a boss or to give unselfishly to meet the needs of a spouse. This discipline is first learned through obedience to parents.

- *the pleasure of doing the right thing*. God has designed us so that we experience joy when we do what is right. Your son or daughter will never admit there was a tiny burst of satisfaction that came when they obeyed

your request and took out the trash, but it is there
nevertheless.

• *the promise of God's blessing for following him.* God's
command to obey comes with the promise of both
quality and quantity of life: "so that you may live
long and that it may go well with you in the land"
(Deuteronomy 5:16). We don't need a scientific study
to see that children who obey generally face fewer
troubles and life-threatening circumstances of their
own making than children who rebel. The promise
of blessing is also experienced in our relationship
with God. The life of faith is a life of dependence on
God's promises. For children, this begins with simple
obedience. In ways that go to the depths of their
souls, they will see God's blessings in their lives as we
encourage them to make this choice.

As they obey their parents in their actions, children also
must treat parents with *honor* in their attitudes. "The command says, 'Honor your father and mother'" (Ephesians 6:2
NCV). Honor and obedience are what children do as they
do their part to help make families work. For some of you,
this is where Bibleland meets Fantasyland. You struggle
to get your children to even speak to you, let alone honor
you. You can't help but think, "If only my kids would act
this way, of course our family would be better—but this
just isn't realistic in my world." These actions and attitudes
don't happen automatically; they rarely happen easily and
never happen perfectly. Yet obedience and honor to parents
are crucial building blocks to success in life, and they are
worth the struggle. If you have young kids, teaching children to honor and obey you is one of your greatest tasks.

What do you do in a family where the honor isn't there, and your kids don't want to do anything you say? Keep fighting. Instead of fighting with them, fight *for* them — for what you know is right. You're not just fighting to get your way; you're fighting for their future. Keep encouraging them to obey; keep asking them to honor. One of the most important things you can do is to find other parents who are fighting for the same thing. A support group or small group of other parents who will listen to you, pray with you, and rejoice with you is vital.

Even for us as adults, there is something about honoring our parents that makes a difference in us. The command to obey our parents stops when we leave our childhood behind, yet we're clearly always to honor our parents. Even when we can't honor their actions, we can honor the fact that they are our parents. One of the greatest lessons we give our kids will be how we treat our parents. This has been a hard truth to accept as I've walked through the struggles with my dad I talked about in our second week. Because of mental issues and alcohol issues in his life and the resulting discomfort and fear I allowed into my life, we found ourselves disconnected on and off for years. It would have been easy to give up on the relationship — sometimes it even seemed like the right thing to do. One day I realized that my kids were watching how I loved my dad. I wanted them to see I was struggling to honor him, not pretending everything was good when it wasn't, not accepting hurts without dealing with them, but struggling to honor my dad as my dad. For me, it meant continuing to write and to try to connect even when it seemed impossible. You may have a parent who is angry or toxically controlling to the point that even connecting is unhealthy right now. You can still honor them as your parent by praying for them in the presence of your children.

According to God, job one for children is obeying and honoring their parents. As parents, we cannot treat our kids any better than to teach and encourage them toward these life-developing actions and attitudes.

### Response from the Heart of a Mom

*Watching Tom struggle with how to honor his dad even in a difficult relationship has inspired me. It is possible to honor someone even when you don't agree with what he or she is doing. From my side as a parent, teaching our children to honor and obey us is just plain hard work sometimes. It seems easier to let it slide, and it can feel like it has a self-centered tone to it, but God clearly commands it. And he surely knows about the value of honoring parents.*

### WEEK 6, DAY 26: How Your Kids Treat You

- **Verse to remember:** "Treat others as you want them to treat you" (Luke 6:31 LB).

- **Action to take:** Encourage honor in your children by making the choice to honor your own parents this week through praying for them, connecting with them in some way, or doing something for them.

- **Tomorrow:** How you treat your kids

# How You Treat
# Your Kids

Many people miss the point of the Golden Rule, which is to treat another person as we want to be treated. It's not about giving someone else the things that would meet my needs; it's about giving them what would most meet *their* needs. Since no one knows and understands our needs better than God, understanding what he says about our relationships is a key to living the Golden Rule. For parents, this means we must understand how God wants children to treat us, namely, with obedience and honor. It also means we must understand how God wants parents to treat children.

If we had to boil down to a single word what God says about how we are to treat our children, it would be the word *nurture*. We touched on this word briefly in an earlier chapter. When we nurture, we set up the right environment for growth. We cannot cause growth in our children; only God can do that. But we can *nurture* growth. Your child's physical growth is caused by the fact that they are a creation of God, made to grow to adulthood. A parent can't cause the growth, but we certainly do nurture it by providing food and making sure our kids get enough exercise and rest.

The same is true spiritually. The environment is all-important! A poor family environment can produce children who, like plants choked by weeds, are being stifled by worries and stress. There are other environments just as unhealthy for growth: hothouse children, who look great in the protected environment but wilt when they get outside into the real world; or Bonsai-tree children, with their roots clipped so carefully that they end up looking like a perfect miniature of their parents' wishes.

In a garden, there are a thousand things to do yet only a few simple principles to follow: water, feed, protect, and weed. In that sense, gardening is a great picture for us as parents. Our days are filled with the actions of parenting, and there are a few simple principles that cause us to be nurturing in these actions.

## 1. Treat your children as a *gift* from God.

Psalm 127:3—a verse we looked at on our first day together—reads, "Children are a gift from the LORD; babies are a reward" (NCV). Many a parent getting up with their child for the tenth time in the night has thought, "If this is the reward, what's the punishment?" Yet for all of the genuine hassles and heartaches of parenting, something in us cannot help but see the gift that children truly are.

I find the strength and wisdom to be a nurturing parent as I remember what a wonderful gift my children are—a gift from God. Reminding ourselves of the miracle of creation and birth has the power to keep this truth in our minds. So keep those baby pictures and ultrasound images; you may need them when you're in a battle of wills with your fourteen-year-old!

Chaundel and I were made aware of the miracle of birth

in ways we never would have chosen. As a young couple, we were soon ready to begin a family; but we waited and waited—and no family came. We eventually went in for tests and were told by the doctors that we would not be able to have children. It was confusing, devastating news for us. As we were praying about medical options, Chaundel became pregnant, and we were filled with joy as we anticipated the arrival of a baby. Our hopes turned again to an even deeper confusion when we suffered a miscarriage of that baby. This seemed like our only chance to have a child. What was God doing? We began to consider adoption, which is a miracle all its own. But this was not God's path for us, as Chaundel became pregnant again. God eventually brought one, then two, then three children into our lives. As our children were growing up, we loved to tell our church, "When we look at our kids we think, 'Look at the wonderful things that God can do.' Now, that's not what we think *every* time we look at our children!" Having to wait for children whom we thought we would never have has kept the miracle of birth always near the surface.

## 2. Treat your children as a *stewardship* from God.

The word *steward* means "manager"; a *stewardship* is something that God has given us to manage well. We most often think of stewardship as related to our money; yet, as important as money is, many things we manage are more important than our finances. The way we manage our time, our words, our relationships—these all have a greater impact than our budget. Your children are a far greater stewardship from God than your money, but which do you take more time to measure and secure? We would never look at our money and think, "It'll turn out just fine," because we know how easily it can be lost or wasted—but sometimes we slip into doing this with our kids.

We manage our time through a schedule, our money through a budget. What is the right tool for managing our children as a stewardship from God? It's *love*. Money is protected by putting it in a bank account; children are stewarded by love. Remember the teaching of 1 Corinthians 13 from day five of our first week: without love it all comes out to nothing. Of course we should plan for the best education of our children; without a doubt we should help them learn important life skills—but without love we can end up treating them as if they were on an assembly line. With love, we are treating them as we would want to be treated as we steward them as unique creations of God.

## 3. Treat your children as *brothers and sisters*.

One of the goals of parenting is that your physical son or daughter becomes your spiritual brother or sister in faith. God tells us that as believers we stand equally before Jesus as brothers and sisters. We all know that our children must have a faith of their own, not a faith that is attached to ours.

This is a belief that gets challenged in the realities of life. Ask yourself:

- Am I OK with my children dealing with doubts, without my being embarrassed that their doubts might reflect badly on me?

- Can I allow my children to take the lead in what we do or how we do our family devotions without my feeling I have to be in control?

- Do I see my child's prayers as simply cute or as meaningful expressions of trust in God?

- As my children grow, am I willing for them to risk a disappointment as they serve others without my feeling I must protect them from any possible hurt?

My answers to these questions reveal whether I'm growing in my spiritual relationship with my children, whether I am seeing them as children of God.

Don't miss the great joy we anticipate as we nurture our children. As Paul talked to his brothers and sisters, he looked forward to one day standing in the presence of God with them: "After all, what gives us hope and joy, and what is our proud reward and crown? It is you! Yes, you will bring us much joy as we stand together before our Lord Jesus when he comes back again. For you are our pride and joy" (1 Thessalonians 2:19 – 20 NLT). Parenting is all about looking forward to that day with your children. The ultimate moment in parenting is not the first day of kindergarten, as poignant as that is; it is not your son's or daughter's wedding day, as wonderful as that can be. The ultimate moment is experienced as you stand together as brother and sister in the presence of Jesus, the one who loves us most.

### *Response from the Heart of a Mom*

*Psalm 127:3 has been written on my heart since the moment Tom and I began trying to have kids. What a gift our children have been and continue to be! I have to stop often and look carefully at how I am managing that gift and at whether I am keeping an eternal perspective. Recently when Alyssa was home briefly from Rwanda, we were at church together. I was so enjoying worshiping with her and lamenting to God that I was afraid there would not be many opportunities for this in her lifetime. He whispered to me, "You have all of eternity to enjoy this gift of worshiping with Alyssa. Let me place her where I will for this life."*

WEEK 6, DAY 27: **How You Treat Your Kids**

- **Verse to remember:** "Children are a gift from the LORD; babies are a reward" (Psalm 127:3 NCV).

- **Action to take:** Take a moment right now, regardless of the circumstances you are facing with your child, to thank God for his gift of that child.

- **Tomorrow:** No such thing as a perfect family

# No Such Thing as a Perfect Family

To live out the Golden Rule in our families, we must meet one another's needs. What do we do when the gold tarnishes? Parents are to give nurture to their children; children are to love and honor their parents. In a perfect world, this would always work out perfectly, but we do not live in a perfect world. I want to take a few moments today to deal with those times when we struggle as parents. When you face struggles, remember that you are not alone. Families have always had issues, even some of the most famous families in the Bible.

Put yourself in the sandals of King David — the same David who killed Goliath and wrote Psalm 23 — as he waited for news of his son Absalom.

Absalom had betrayed his father by trying to take his kingdom. David certainly could have seen that he himself had planted some of the seeds of this betrayal — sins David had committed against his family, mistakes of overpermissiveness he had made, the times he had ignored his children because of the stresses of running a kingdom. David may have planted some seeds, but Absalom made the choice to allow these seeds to grow. Because of his selfish desire to enjoy the luxuries of power and his openness to listening to advisers who appealed to his pride, Absalom had successfully pushed his father out of the capital city and had taken his throne for a time.

David responded with humble trust instead of arrogant anger. Reduced to life's basics, he and his small group of supporters lived for a time in the countryside, living in simple dependence on God's daily supply. Perhaps David wondered if God was choosing to raise up his son Absalom to replace him as leader. It soon became evident that Absalom could not effectively rule out of his spirit of anger and indulgence. His kingdom began to implode.

David and his followers recaptured the throne, and now Absalom was being chased down. David wanted his son brought before him, but not for revenge. He wanted to express forgiveness to his child. He hoped beyond hope for a reconciliation. David had made huge mistakes in his own life; he knew that God can forgive and restore.

Then the news came. Absalom had been killed. David was devastated. Every parent feels the torture in David's cry: "O my son Absalom! My son, my son Absalom!" David's son had betrayed him, but David never stopped loving his son. When Absalom died, instead of choosing to distance himself emotionally, David poured out his heart in an expression of grief and loss. It is the story of an imperfect father, a selfish son, a tragic end—and a continuing choice to love. (From 2 Samuel 15–19.)

A parent once wrote me: "There is a verse in the Bible that causes me a great deal of shame or pain or guilt—I really don't know which! 'Train a child in the way he should go, and when he is old he will not turn from it' [Proverbs

22:6]. One of my children has not gone to church since she left our home. She is living a very rebellious life, and I can't help but feel this verse is telling me that if I had just trained her right, this would not be happening."

This great proverb has been the source of more heartache than you can imagine. I hope we can begin today to heal some of that hurt. Here is the pattern that leads to the heartache. Even when our kids are small, we begin to worry about whether they will make the right choices in life. As Christian parents we'd like to have a *guarantee* that our kids will follow God even more fully than we have. With this desire in our hearts, we come across this verse and think, "That's it! God has promised that I'll always have great children."

But then *it* happens. Your child has a rough time in middle school, high school, or college. They fall in with the wrong friends, and the heart for God that you had hoped and prayed for them is nowhere to be seen. Then comes the thought that brings the heartache: "If God promised that if only I would raise my child right, they wouldn't turn away —what's wrong? God's promise can't fail, so maybe there *is* something wrong with the way I raised my child." We may never voice this thought to anyone, but nevertheless it is there, not far below the surface.

Let me say three things to those who struggle with this thought—or to pass along to someone who is hurting:

1. In this world, there is no such thing as a perfect parent. This proverb is not about guaranteeing that your kids will turn out perfectly if you're perfect; nor is it about blaming yourself for the fact that you are less than perfect. We live in an imperfect world.

2. In heaven, there is a perfect Parent. God's actions toward us are always perfect, never selfish, and filled with constant love. Yet look at how many of his children have turned away from that love. It started in the garden of Eden. If God's perfect love toward us cannot guarantee that none of his children will ever fall away, how can we place that burden on our parenting? Your teaching cannot violate their free will to choose the right or wrong any more than God's direction could keep Adam and Eve from eating the fruit on the tree from which he had commanded them not to eat.

3. What, then, does this proverb mean? As with most of the book of Proverbs, it expresses a universal principle, not an individual promise. Nine times out of ten (more like 99 times out of 100), if you teach the right thing, your kids will end up doing the right thing. That is God's moral law. And don't miss the phrase "when he is *old* he will not turn from it." *Old* means old. It doesn't mean sixteen or even twenty-six years of age; it means old. The truth is, those good lessons you taught *were* heard; they did sink in. Stop telling yourself that the time you gave to teaching your child was "just wasted." Those teachings sunk in so deeply that even when your child is old, maybe even after you are gone, they will emerge again to give your grown son or daughter the direction they need.

What do you do in the meantime as you go through the struggle with your child? "Treat others as you want them to treat you." One of the greatest choices you can make to live out the Golden Rule toward your children is in the three words "don't give up." You don't want people to give up on you; your children need you to not give up on them. You may think, "Of course I won't give up on my kids; that's what it means to be a parent!" Even if this seems obvious, don't miss the significance. It is an awesome gift to have one person in your life who you know will never give up on you. Every one of us has this guarantee in Jesus' love (Hebrews 13:5); some of us also have this guarantee in another person.

The problem as we seek not to give up, of course, is that we get weary. We don't want to give up, but sometimes we feel too worn-out to go on. This is true even in the simple things. We feel like we just can't change one more dirty diaper; we want to give up and go to bed when that school art project just isn't coming together. Our weariness also hits in more significant ways; for instance, we feel we just don't have it in us to keep hoping our child will reconnect with us.

Although the rewards of parenting can be great, the work is often wearying. The hours are 24/7. You don't get a scheduled week off, day off, or even a lunch break! Even when you are not with your children, you are still thinking about them. Add to this the fact that one of your children is now struggling, and of course you wonder where you can find the strength to go on loving. I certainly don't know all of the answers to the hurt you are now facing with your child, and I have found that those with easy answers to life-long problems are often the most hurtful of all. I do know we don't find the strength to parent in ourselves; I know we need a hope and power beyond ourselves to love our children. And I do know that you are not alone in the struggle. I often need to hear Jesus personally whispering the words,

"Come to me, all of you who are weary and carry heavy burdens, and I will give you rest" (Matthew 11:28 NLT). I know how often I feel like giving up, even in the little things—and I've found that the only way not to give up is by not going it alone. Parent together with Jesus. Ask for his rest when you're weary. Let him carry the burden that is too heavy, and choose to come to him daily to receive his encouraging strength.

### Response from the Heart of a Mom

*My parents' hearts were broken when my brother, Jim, walked away from God. It seemed he would never return, despite countless prayers and a happy, secure upbringing. It was only after they were both in heaven that we had the joy of seeing Jim fully recommit to the Lord and find the joy and purpose that had been lacking for much of his life. They are now reunited in heaven, celebrating how great our heavenly Father is.*

### WEEK 6, DAY 28: No Such Thing as a Perfect Family

- **Verse to remember:** "Come to me, all of you who are weary and carry heavy burdens, and I will give you rest" (Matthew 11:28 NLT).

- **Action to take:** Worship God by letting go of your false image of perfection and trusting in his power to work in your life today.

- **Tomorrow:** A Father like no other

# A Father Like No Other

A Christian psychologist shares a technique he occasionally uses in counseling:

> Sometimes I ask people who are having a difficult time describing their God to draw a picture of him. As you might imagine, I have an interesting collection of drawings. Several depict a huge eye which covers a whole page—God watching everything they do, waiting to catch them at some failure or wrongdoing. Others have drawn angry human faces, or birds of prey with sharp beaks and talons. One young theological student said he couldn't draw very well but next time he'd bring a picture of his God. I was very curious about it. It happened to be the Christmas season and he brought a magazine with an artist's drawing of an extra large, angry, and demanding Scrooge sitting behind a desk, quill pen in hand with his debit-credit ledger before him. Standing in front of the desk facing Scrooge was small, terror-stricken Bob Cratchit. Pointing to Scrooge he explained, "That's God," and then to Cratchit, "That's

me." And just think, this young seminarian made an A in his theology class!*

A.W. Tozer once wrote, "What comes into our minds when we think about God is the most important thing about us."†

The most important thing about you as a parent is how you respond to God as your Father. A false image of God impacts our hearts more than we can imagine. If you think of God as angry, you may feel justified about adopting a pattern of anger in your life; or, more often than not, you will react against this false image and become overly permissive. We will either react with or react against our false images of God.

To live out the reality of the Golden Rule in our families, we need a power that is beyond ourselves. Left to myself, I'm much more concerned about how you should treat me than about how I should be treating you. There is no more significant choice you can make as a mother or father than to trust God as your Father. While we surely cannot cover an entire theology of God in one day's reading, I want to point in the direction of a trust in God that will impact every day of our parenting. God desires to be a Father to us. We have to learn to trust him as our Father.

I have found that many who believe in Jesus for their salvation have never really learned how to let God be Father. They may know how to believe in him as Creator, Savior, and Judge but not as Father. Jesus taught us to pray, "Our Father in heaven," because he knew how important this trust is to our daily lives. If you grew up with an absent or abusive

---

*David Seamands, *Healing of Memories* (Wheaton, Ill.: Victor, 1985), 100–101.

†A. W. Tozer, *Knowledge of the Holy* (New York: Harper, 1961), 9.

earthly father, great blessings come to your life and your parenting as you trust God as the Father you never had.

In an acrostic based on the word *FATHER*, we will consider six ways we can trust God today as a parent and in every other area of our lives:

## Feel his compassion.

This is where it begins. I have to know God cares about me. How can I have any kind of relationship with someone who doesn't care about me? "He is like a father to us, tender and sympathetic to those who reverence him" (Psalm 103:13 LB). God cares; he understands our problems, our pain, our potential. *Compassion* means "to feel with." God is not simply watching us; he has compassion for what we are facing today.

Some think that because God is all-knowing, he cannot have genuine compassion. They picture God watching our lives in the same way we might watch a movie for the tenth time — not caring in the same way because he knows the end of the story. The depths of the heart of God are more than we can understand. *He* may know the end of the story, but he knows that *we* don't.

How do you feel this compassion in your daily life? The answer is in the verse we just looked at: *reverence him*. One definition of *reverence* is "awe-filled awareness of God" — awareness that God cares, really cares, about what is happening in your life at this moment. For many this sense of reverence comes through listening to Christian music alone or singing with others; for others, this reverent understanding of the compassion of God can come as they slowly read through the book of Psalms and come across Psalm 23 or verses such as Psalm 103:8 – 10:

> The LORD is compassionate and gracious,
> 'slow to anger, abounding in love.
> He will not always accuse,
>   nor will he harbor his anger forever;
> he does not treat us as our sins deserve
>   or repay us according to our iniquities.

## Accept his unconditional love.

The famous interviewer Larry King jokes that the one interview he'd still like to do is one with God. Then he says, "First question: Did you have a son, because a lot is riding on the answer?"*

*Everything* rides on that answer, which is why Jesus came to this earth to show us the love of God as expressed through his Son. Jesus demonstrated that love through his teaching and miracles, through his death and resurrection. This is why John 3:16 is such a famous verse, because it so clearly proclaims God's unconditional love for each of us: "For God so loved the world that he gave his one and only Son, that whoever believes in him shall not perish but have eternal life" (John 3:16). In 1 John 3:1 (LB), John writes, "See how very much our heavenly Father loves us, for he allows us to be called his children—think of it—and we really *are!*"

I cannot get for myself what can only be given by God. I can search my whole life, looking to parents, friends, spouse, children. No human being can meet my need for unconditional love. Because I am a creation of God, there is a God-sized need in the middle of my heart. You begin by accepting God's love through the gift of grace in Jesus in a

---

*Larry King and Pat Piper, *Anything Goes!* (New York: Warner, 2000), 181.

simple prayer of grateful commitment. Then comes the life of faith as you live in daily trust in the unconditional love of your Father.

## Tell him your needs.

God loves me unconditionally. Once I accept this love, I need to take the next step in my relationship with him — begin telling him what I need. This may sound simple, yet I know many who have been believers for a long time who haven't taken this next step in letting God be their Father. How can we trust God for our salvation — our greatest need — and then not trust him to meet our daily needs? It doesn't make sense, yet we often find ourselves doing just that. Jesus said, "Your Father knows what you need before you ask him. This, then, is how you should pray: 'Our Father in heaven, hallowed be your name ...'" (Matthew 6:8–9). We talk to God as a Father out of a belief that he knows what we need. The obvious question is: If he knows what I need, why do I need to ask? You're not asking to inform God of your need; you're asking to *depend* on God for that need. As you ask, remember that you're talking to a Father who wants to give to his children. Jesus said, "If you, then, though you are evil, know how to give good gifts to your children, how much more will your Father in heaven give good gifts to those who ask him!" (Matthew 7:11).

## Heed his guidance.

"The LORD says, 'I will make you wise and show you where to go. I will guide you and watch over you'" (Psalm 32:8 NCV). God gives wisdom that results in direction for life. I'm trusting God as my Father when I allow this wisdom to guide me in the right direction. This can be the most difficult part of trusting God as your Father. We want to go our own way, not always because we're self-seeking but often because we can see our way more clearly. It's hard to trust what you cannot see.

A bird flew into our house through the patio door a few days ago. As it tried to find its way out, it came upon a fixed pane window and flew against it again and again. I found a broom and began to gently sweep the bird toward the open door. As I did this, I thought, "I wonder what the bird thinks of this broom."

This is a parable of our lives. We keep beating our heads against what seems to be the only way out, the only visible answer—so the pane window becomes the pain window! God comes along and begins to sweep us in the right direction, but the broom looks terrifying. "What are you doing, God?" we think. "You're pushing me away from the only obvious way out of this." The truth is, *God knows* where the open doors are to be found, so we need to trust his guidance.

## Enjoy his presence.

Trusting God as your Father means more than relying on his provision and direction; it also means simply enjoying being in the presence of the one who loves you the most. You are now close to God. "But now in Christ Jesus, you who were far away from God are brought near through the blood of Christ's death" (Ephesians 2:13 NCV). You are now taught to pray to God as your *"Abba*, Father." "You did not receive a spirit that makes you a slave again to fear, but you received the Spirit of sonship. And by him we cry, 'Abba, Father'" (Romans 8:15). *Abba* is the Aramaic word like our word *Daddy*, the most intimate name for a father, a name a little child would use.

Visiting Israel years ago, I was, of course, deeply impacted by the significance of being in the places where the events of the Bible had taken place. I think, however, that the most powerful moment came not at the pool of Siloam or the Garden Tomb but in a city park. As we ate lunch, we watched children and families play. A preschool boy spotted his father on the other side of the park and ran full speed toward him, crying out, *"Abba, Abba, Abba,"* all the way. It was an unforgettable picture of the intimacy and closeness I have with God as my Father.

The popular idea is that God is distant; the real truth is that *God is near.* He is as near as your next heartbeat, your every thought. The popular idea is that God watches over our actions; the real truth is that God is intimately involved in *every detail* of our lives. The popular idea is that God is eagerly waiting to judge those who do wrong; the real truth is that God is waiting to forgive all who ask (1 Timothy 2:4). In a world in which people see God as unapproachable, the real truth is that God is relational.

## Rejoice in his reward.

If I say to you, "God saw what you did last week," how does that make you feel? Many of us struggle with feelings of guilt and shame, and there is no doubt we are in need of God's forgiveness. Yet Jesus looked at things entirely differently. He said, "Your Father can see what is done in secret, and he will reward you" (Matthew 6:4 NCV). God saw the good choices you made that grew out of your faith in Jesus, and your Father is looking to reward you. We have a difficult time getting past the feeling that God is out to get us, when the truth is that he is waiting to take joy in us. Paul writes, "You are no longer a slave, but a son; and since you are a son, God has made you also an heir" (Galatians 4:7). You are part of the family, part of the inheritance. Trusting God as Father means looking forward to the reward he so graciously will give: "Without faith it is impossible to please God, because anyone who comes to him must believe that he exists and that he rewards those who earnestly seek him" (Hebrews 11:6).

Trust God as your Father. This goes right to the core of our parenting. For some, trusting God is easy, because you grew up with a loving and compassionate father for a role model. Thank God for this gift! For others, trusting God as a Father is difficult because you had a distant or even cruel father growing up. A refreshing breakthrough may occur as you begin to see God as the Father you never had, to see God as the Father who fulfills what your father never was.

One thing you can do to give your life a new perspective is to pray the following prayer. Pray the parts appropriate for your life, and add to the prayer where you need to:

*God, I now accept you as the Father I never had. I was disappointed by my father, but you will never disappoint me. I never knew my earthly father, but I do know you. I was hurt by my earthly father, but I am healed by you. I was ignored by my earthly father, but I have your full and constant attention. I could never meet the expectations of my earthly father, but I can find freedom from expectations in your grace. In Jesus' name, amen.*

### Response from the Heart of a Mom

*I am constantly trying to realign my view of God with what the Bible teaches. This chapter is a good reminder about many aspects of who God really is as my Father. I love remembering that God sees all of our work, even that which no one else sees. Especially as a mom whose babies were not very good at sleeping, I find comfort in remembering that God saw and supported me all those nights I had to get up with them—and through the countless other things I did for our children that maybe weren't noticed by anyone else but my heavenly Father.*

WEEK 6, DAY 29: **A Father Like No Other**

- **Verse to remember:** "You did not receive a spirit that makes you a slave again to fear, but you received the Spirit of sonship. And by him we cry, '*Abba*, Father'" (Romans 8:15).

- **Action to take:** Take a moment right now to think about God's compassion for a situation that you are facing.

- **Tomorrow:** Trusting God for the impossible

# Trusting God for the Impossible

Congratulations. You've made it to the end of this thirty-day journey. On our last day, I want to focus on one of my favorite encouragements for parents—the words spoken to Mary, the mother of Jesus, by an angel: "Nothing is impossible with God" (Luke 1:37 NLT). I'll admit freely that none of us will face the challenge that Mary was facing that day as she sought to understand the promise of a virgin birth. Yet we face the same feelings of confusion and fear in our parenting, and we need to hear the same promise.

> Parents wondering if they'll be up to welcoming a new baby into their home need to hear, "Nothing is impossible with God."

> A mom and dad struggling with how to help a child with a learning disability need to know, "Nothing is impossible with God."

> Parents feeling overwhelmed by the constant challenges of their preschooler need to hold on to this truth: "Nothing is impossible with God."

A mom or dad dealing with the raging hormones of their teenager needs to know, "Nothing is impossible with God."

Parents feeling heartbroken at releasing their adult children need to see, "Nothing is impossible with God."

A single parent wondering where she will get the strength for one more day needs to feel, "Nothing is impossible with God."

*All* parents, knowing that the job is still beyond them even when times are good, need to embrace the strong conviction, "Nothing is impossible with God."

How do we trust God for the impossible in our lives? If we want to be great parents, we need to learn from Mary and Joseph, the earthly parents God chose for Jesus. Mary discovered that God can make the impossible possible. We often look at the statistics to measure the possibility of success in our parenting, and statistics and studies can give us some important perspectives. But God is not limited by statistics. What were the odds that a virgin girl from Nazareth would give birth to a son in a stable in Bethlehem?

The life of Mary reveals four stages we go through in trusting God for the impossible. I'm sure you'll be able to relate to these feelings as a parent.

## 1. Our first feeling is fear.

You'll often experience feelings of confusion and even fear in your parenting. The answer is to listen to what God is saying. Don't miss what he is saying about you.

"Greetings, you who are highly favored! The Lord is with you," the angel said to Mary (Luke 1:28). This must have confused her; "highly favored" was commonly addressed to kings and priests, not to common peasant girls. This title just didn't fit Mary's picture of herself. Part of the answer to her fear was recognizing that what God said about her was more real than her opinion of herself.

How about you? How do you picture yourself? Think about how you would feel if God said to you:

- Greetings, loved one!
- Greetings, important one!
- Greetings, useful one!
- Greetings, one whom I've entrusted with the gift of a child!

God says all this about you, and more. This may be the last picture you would ever have of yourself, but remember, "Nothing is impossible with God!"

## 2. It often seems ordinary.

This miracle happened in such an ordinary way. Jesus was born as a baby, in a stable no less. How ordinary can you get! Wouldn't you have expected God to make his entrance in a more spectacular way? These days a new diaper is introduced into the world with press conferences, social networking campaigns, and millions of dollars in advertising. Jesus was born in the usual way in a pretty much ignored corner of his world.

God makes the impossible possible, often in the most "ordinary" of ways. While we wait for the fireworks, God is patiently working in the trenches. An ordinary feeding of strained peas to your baby, an ordinary reading of a story at bedtime, an ordinary leading of a school field trip—and all of a sudden we discover that God is doing something extraordinary!

Despite the drudgery, God is working. "Nothing is impossible with God."

## 3. It usually brings more problems at first.

Could problems and struggles ever be a part of the impossible becoming possible? Just ask Joseph and Mary! They immediately faced an unexplained pregnancy, a terribly timed trip to Bethlehem, no room in the inn, labor in a stable, no crib but a feeding trough for the new baby! All of the problems did not make the slightest dent in God's miracle. In fact, some of the struggles were a direct result of their involvement in the impossible. This struggle in the midst of miracles is the rule rather than the exception in the Bible.

There is no doubt that becoming parents will bring more problems into our lives, not less. Our problems do not prohibit God's possibilities. We think the minute we run into a problem we've lost all hope. The truth is, if the impossible is to become possible in your life, there will certainly be some problems along the way. God can be at work even in the midst of your struggles and fears. "Nothing is impossible with God."

## 4. It is a matter of faith!

Where do you find the faith to be a parent? I can think of no better way to encourage you as we come to the end of this thirty-day journey than to share three places where you can find day-to-day faith. First, *look within you*. Mary was told, "The Holy Spirit will come upon you" (Luke 1:35).

Parenting involves every moment of every day, so you need power from God for every moment of every day. That is what his Spirit desires to give you. Your family life does not have to be determined by how you were raised—not if you are filled with God's Spirit. It does not have to be governed by how things have been, not if you are filled with God's Spirit. It does not have to be limited to what it is now, not if you are filled with God's Spirit.

Look within you, and then *look around you*. Look to see whom God has put into your life—someone who can be a support and encouragement. For Mary, it was her relative Elizabeth, who was pregnant with John the Baptist at the time. No one was facing the same experience as Mary, yet she was able to find someone who was experiencing enough of the same circumstances to be a support. Although you will never find anyone who is facing exactly the same life situations you face, you can always find those who can relate and encourage.

Look within you, look around you, and *look above you*. The angel directed Mary's attention to God because God is greater, far greater, than any opportunity or problem you will ever encounter as a parent.

> Praise the LORD, I tell myself;
>     O LORD my God, how great you are!
> You are robed with honor and with majesty;
>     you are dressed in a robe of light.
> You stretch out the starry curtain of the heavens;
>     you lay out the rafters of your home in the rain clouds.
> You make the clouds your chariots;
>     you ride upon the wings of the wind.
>
> PSALM 104:1–3 NLT

Nothing is impossible with God!

Mary chose to trust in God, and that trust led her to places she never could have imagined. Her trust led her to a barn in Bethlehem, and to an exile in Egypt to protect the baby Jesus. Her trust led her to temporarily losing Jesus at the temple when he was twelve years old, to being present at his first miracle when he was thirty years old, and to watching him die a cruel death on a cross when he was thirty-three years old. Her trust in God led her to an empty tomb and a resurrected Jesus and to an upper room and the beginning of the church.

You have no idea where your trust in God will lead you as a parent. You cannot control the circumstances. You can be confident that no matter the circumstances, God will be with you and will strengthen you for each day. You cannot always will your child to do as you want. You can be sure that God will pour his love through you to your child. You cannot guarantee the future. You can be convinced that the God of the universe has the future firmly in his hand.

### Response from the Heart of a Mom

*Mary's example of surrender and trust is a daily challenge to me—especially as a parent. I don't think I would have responded as she did when the angel came to her: "I am the Lord's servant, and I am willing to accept whatever he wants" (Luke 1:38 NLT). But this has become my daily prayer and a perspective I strive for. If I can approach all I do in parenting as God's servant, it sheds a whole different light on what seems like an impossible task. I get to be the short-term manager, but they really are his children, after all!*

WEEK 6, DAY 30: **Trusting God for the Impossible**

- **Verse to remember:** "Nothing is impossible with God" (Luke 1:37 NLT).

- **Action to take:** Love your kids the way Jesus loves you, one day at a time!

# Afterword

As we come to the end of our study, I encourage you to read again the six principles we have examined. Read them with the thought strongly in your mind, "Nothing is impossible with God."

## RELATIONSHIP PRINCIPLE #1: Place the Highest Value on Relationships

"The most important command is this: 'Listen, people of Israel! The Lord our God is the only Lord. Love the Lord your God with all your heart, all your soul, all your mind, and all your strength.' The second command is this: 'Love your neighbor as you love yourself.' There are no commands more important than these."

MARK 12:29–31 NCV

## RELATIONSHIP PRINCIPLE #2: Love as Jesus Loves You

"A new command I give you: Love one another. As I have loved you, so you must love one another."

JOHN 13:34

RELATIONSHIP PRINCIPLE #3: **Communicate from the Heart**

"For out of the overflow of the heart the mouth speaks."

MATTHEW 12:34

RELATIONSHIP PRINCIPLE #4: **As You Judge, You Will Be Judged**

"Do not judge, or you too will be judged. For in the same way you judge others, you will be judged, and with the measure you use, it will be measured to you."

MATTHEW 7:1–2

RELATIONSHIP PRINCIPLE #5: **The Greatest Are the Servants**

"The greatest among you will be your servant. For whoever exalts himself will be humbled, and whoever humbles himself will be exalted."

MATTHEW 23:11–12

RELATIONSHIP PRINCIPLE #6: **Treat Others as You Want Them to Treat You**

"Do to others as you would have them do to you."

LUKE 6:31

# Bible Versions Cited

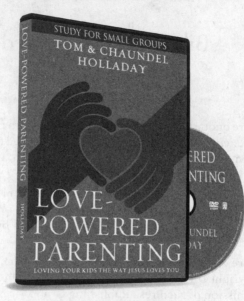

# The Relationship Principles of Jesus

*Tom Holladay, teaching pastor, Saddleback Church*

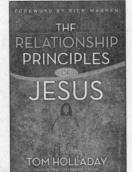

What would you give to radically improve, even transform, what matters most in your relationships?

How about forty days of your time?

In forty days, bring new depth and health to your marriage, your family, and your friendships. In six weeks you'll explore and implement six foundational principles that Jesus taught and lived. You'll be equipped with insights and a practical path for fulfilling God's intention for all your relationships—even the difficult ones.

Shaped after Rick Warren's monumental bestseller, *The Purpose Driven® Life*, this book invites you to learn from the Master of relationships. *The Relationship Principles of Jesus* will profoundly shape how you view relationships.

*Available wherever books are sold!*

# Foundations*

## 11 Core Truths to Build Your Life On

*Tom Holladay and Kay Warren*

Ideal for Sunday night or midweek series, weekday Bible Studies, Sunday school classes, and study groups of any size

Give your church members the key that can:

- enable them to see how beliefs change behavior
- lessen their day-to-day stress level
- increase their security in an insecure world
- help them raise their kids with a right perspective on life
- increase their love for and trust in God

The twenty-four sessions in *Foundations* will take you for thought-provoking, life-changing explorations of eleven core Christian truths:

1. The Bible
2. God
3. Jesus
4. The Holy Spirit
5. Creation
6. Salvation
7. Sanctification
8. Good and Evil
9. The Afterlife
10. The Church
11. The Second Coming

Everything you need is provided, with tools, tips, and options to help you meet the unique needs of your group.

- **Teaching notes** — Extensive notes guide you through what you will say and include illustrations and applications of each doctrine under discussion.
- **Highlight sections** — Four kinds of sidebars help your group connect with God's truths through key words, thought-provoking insights, personal implications, and personal applications.

*A Purpose-Driven® Discipleship Resource

- **Teaching tips** — Over sixty proven tips help you strengthen your skills as a communicator.
- **Discussion questions** — Questions at the end of each study can also be interspersed throughout the lesson.
- **Split-session plan** — Each lesson has a cutoff point that allows you to break it into two sessions. Subdivide a single lesson or several lessons, or break the entire program into forty-six lessons at your discretion.
- **Appendixes** — Additional supporting material for some studies may be found at the end of those studies.
- **Memory cards** — Reproducible cards contain a key theme and verse for each of the eleven doctrines covered.
- **PowerPoint slides** — Slides to guide the participants through each of the twenty-four sessions are included on the CD-ROM
- **Additional resources** — CD-ROM contains additional handouts and supplemental programming resources that may be printed out and used.

This is a proven, tested curriculum that has helped change thousands of lives!

For the past ten years, *Foundations* has been used as the doctrinal course at Saddleback Church, one of America's largest and best-known churches. Thousands of Saddleback members have benefited from this life-transforming experience. This course is explained in detail in Rick Warren's groundbreaking book, *The Purpose Driven Church*. Purpose Driven churches all around the world are using *Foundations* to raise up an army of mature believers equipped for ministry in the church and prepared for mission in the world.

*Foundations* **kit includes:**
- 2 Teacher's Guides (volumes 1 and 2)
- 1 Participant's Guide
- 1 CD-ROM with PowerPoint presentations, programming resources, and additional handouts

*Available wherever books are sold!*

# Foundations

## 11 Core Truths to Build Your Life On

*Taught by Tom Holladay and Kay Warren*

Foundations is a series of 11 four-week video studies covering the most important, foundational doctrines of the Christian faith. Study topics include:

### The Bible

This study focuses on where the Bible came from, why it can be trusted, and how it can change your life.

### God

This study focuses not just on facts about God, but on how to know God himself in a more powerful and personal way.

### Jesus

As we look at what the Bible says about the person of Christ, we do so as people who are developing a lifelong relationship with Jesus.

### The Holy Spirit

This study focuses on the person, the presence, and the power of the Holy Spirit, and how you can be filled with the Holy Spirit on a daily basis.

### Creation

Each of us was personally created by a loving God. This study does not shy away from the great scientific and theological arguments that surround the creation/evolution debate. However, you will find the goal of this study is deepening your awareness of God as your Creator.

## Salvation

This study focuses on God's solution to man's need for salvation, what Jesus Christ did for us on the cross, and the assurance and security of God's love and provision for eternity.

## Sanctification

This study focuses on the two natures of the Christian. We'll see the difference between grace and law, and how these two things work in our lives.

## Good and Evil

Why do bad things happen to good people? Through this study we'll see how and why God continues to allow evil to exist. The ultimate goal is to build up our faith and relationship with God as we wrestle with these difficult questions.

## The Afterlife

The Bible does not answer all the questions we have about what happens to us after we die; however, this study deals with what the Bible does tell us. This important study gives us hope and helps us move from a focus on the here and now to a focus on eternity.

## The Church

This study focuses on the birth of the church, the nature of the church, and the mission of the church.

## The Second Coming

This study addresses both the hope and the uncertainties surrounding the second coming of Jesus Christ.

*Available wherever books are sold!*

# The Purpose Driven® Life

## What On Earth Am I Here For?

*by Rick Warren*

### A GROUNDBREAKING MANIFESTO ON THE MEANING OF LIFE!

The most basic question everyone faces in life is *Why am I here? What is my purpose?* Self-help books suggest looking within, at your own desires and dreams, but Rick Warren says that is the wrong place to start. You must begin with God — and his eternal purposes for your life. Real meaning and significance don't come from pursuing human goals but from understanding and fulfilling God's purposes for putting you on earth. This book will help you understand God's incredible plan for your life. You'll see "the big picture" of what life is all about and begin to live the life God created you to live.

*The Purpose Driven®* Life is a manifesto for Christian living in the 21st century—a lifestyle based on eternal purposes, not cultural values. Using biblical stories and letting the Bible speak for itself, Warren clearly explains God's five purposes for each of us:

- You were planned for God's pleasure—so your first purpose is to experience *real worship*.
- You were formed for God's family—so your second purpose is to enjoy *real fellowship*.
- You were created to become like Christ—so your third purpose is to learn *real discipleship*.
- You were shaped for serving God—so your fourth purpose is to practice *real ministry*.
- You were made for a mission—so your fifth purpose is to live out *real evangelism*.

Written in a captivating devotional style, the book is divided into 40 short chapters that can be read as a daily devotional, studied by small groups, and used by churches participating in the worldwide 40 Days of Purpose campaign.